Hippocrene International Cookbook Classics
The Best of Smorgasbord Cooking

This new cookbook is the perfect introduction to the recipes of a typical Swedish smorgasbord. The traditional smorgasbord, a large table of hot and cold dishes, is usually offered as a selection of appetizers before a seated dinner. However, with meats, cheeses, salads and fish dishes, a smorgasbord can be a buffet dinner in itself.

The Best of Smorgasbord Cooking includes recipes for meat and game dishes, aspics and salads, fish, pastas and vegetables. It even includes tips for garnishing and serving the foods. These savory tidbits may be used in any combination to create a unique presentation or, when served alone, make excellent luncheon or supper dishes.

Also included are instructions for mixing the cocktails and egg nogs that traditionally accompany a smorgasbord.

HIPPOCRENE INTERNATIONAL COOKBOOK CLASSICS

All Along the Danube by Marina Polvay, $11.95pb

The Art of Brazilian Cookery by Dolores Botafogo, $9.95pb

The Art of Hungarian Cooking by Paula P. Bennett and Velma R. Clark, $8.95pb

The Art of Israeli Cooking by Chef Aldo Nahoum, $8.95pb

The Art of Persian Cooking by Forough Hekmat, $9.95pb

The Art of Syrian Cookery by Helen Corey, $8.95pb

The Art of Turkish Cooking by Neşet Eren, $9.95pb

The Best of Finnish Cooking by Taimi Previdi, $19.95

The Best of Polish Cooking by Karen West, $8.95pb

The Best of Russian Cooking by Alexandra Kropotkin, $9.95pb

The Best of Ukrainian Cuisine by Bohdan Zahny, $19.95

The Honey Cookbook by Maria Lo Pinto, $8.95pb

The Cuisine of Armenia by Sonia Uvezian, $11.95pb

The Joy of Chinese Cooking by Doreen Yen Hung Feng, $8.95pb

A Spanish Family Cookbook by Juan and Susan Serrano, $9.95pb

(All prices subject to change.)

TO PURCHASE HIPPOCRENE BOOKS contact your local bookstore, or write to: HIPPOCRENE BOOKS, 171 Madison Avenue, New York, NY 10016. Please enclose check or money order, adding $5.00 shipping (UPS) for the first book and $.50 for each additional book.

HIPPOCRENE INTERNATIONAL COOKBOOK CLASSICS

The Best of Smorgasbord Cooking

Gerda Simonson

HIPPOCRENE BOOKS
New York

For information, address:
HIPPOCRENE BOOKS, INC.
171 Madison Avenue
New York, NY 10016

ISBN 0-7818-0407-8

Printed in the United States of America.

Swedish
Hors D'Oeuvres
(Smörgåsbord)

For those who are not familiar with the smörgåsbord, I offer this explanation:

In restaurants and hotels in Sweden, you will find a large table laden with from fifteen to fifty varieties of food—mostly cold dishes. There are two or three kinds of herring, three or four kinds of other fish—smoked, pickled, or plain, three to five salads, assorted sausages, headcheese, smoked ham, smoked tongue, roast pork, veal, beef, various egg dishes, chicken and game in Chaufroix, á la daubes in varied forms, and three to five kinds of cheese. There are also from three to five hot dishes described as "Småvarmt"—such as fish or meat au gratin, tiny meat balls "Köttbullar," kidneys, hash, minced chicken, calves' brains, sweetbreads, omelets, etc.

The guests serve themselves from this table to whatever they fancy. It is customary to serve with these hors d'oeuvres cocktails or "Aquavit" (Water of Life) and beer. Too often it is overlooked that the smörgåsbord is but a table of appetizers, after which dinner is served at the dining-table— including soup, fish, meat, salad, and dessert with or without wines, as preferred. Coffee and liqueurs "Kaffe Avec" are served in the lounge or café, where entertainment and dancing often take place. It is a very pleasant custom to thus leisurely enjoy your "Kaffe Avec" and cigarettes while seated in comfortable chairs reading, conversing, or listening to the music.

Most of the recipes in this book are equally as good for luncheon dishes as for the smörgåsbord. You will note that I have included a few Swedish desserts, which may be used after any of the smörgåsbord dishes for luncheon, also hot tidbit suggestions for the increasingly popular cocktail hour.

The famous revolving "SMÖRGÅSBORD" at the Three Crowns Restaurant, New York City, N. Y.

Author's Note

The suggestion has been advanced that these recipes should state how many persons they serve, but as they are written chiefly for "Smörgåsbord", it is a difficult thing to determine. A great deal depends upon how many other dishes are to be served, and also upon the appetites of the guests. With "Smörgåsbord", canapes, sandwiches, a rich soup, etc., the main course of a dinner should be reduced by one-third. On the other hand, if the main course consists of meat or fish with a rich gravy or sauce, together with creamed and other vegetables, naturally the "Smörgåsbord" should not be too elaborate. The richness of the salad and dessert is also governed by what has preceded these courses.

A reasonable schedule keeping the above in mind follows:

1. Boneless meat such as Tenderloin of Beef, Veal, Lamb, smoked Ham, chopped meat, trimmed beef Tongue, Liver etc. 1/3 to ½ lb. per person.

2. Meat with partly bone and fat, Sirloin Steak, Chops, Roast Beef, Leg of Lamb, Fresh Ham, Loin of Pork, meat for stew, etc., ½ to 2/3 lb. per person.

3. Bony and fat meat, Breast or shoulder of Lamb. Veal, Spareribs and Brisket of Beef either fresh or corned at least 1 lb. or more per person.

4. Fowl of all kinds, such as Chicken, Turkey, Squabs, Ducks and Game 1 lb. per person. It is advantageous to prepare a good stuffing and rich gravy, as the bones and intestines which are removed, weigh a great deal.

5. Fish—In buying Fish, the richness in itself must be considered. In addition, Fish served with a rich sauce will of course, go further than plain cooked.

In dealing with a reliable market, one need not hesitate to ask questions. Due to their experience and knowledge of the quality of their own products, one may reasonably depend upon the advice and judgment of such dealers.

Personally, I feel that every woman, as head of the home, should study economy and thereby get the best results.

I have included many recipes using left overs for palatable meals.

I feel indebted to the management of the well known COPENHAGEN RESTAURANT and the THREE CROWNS RESTAURANT in NEW YORK CITY for their splendid cooperation in making up the different dishes and platters which are illustrated in this book. I hope that these photographs will inspire rather than dismay the novice in her preparation of the "Smörgasbord" dishes.

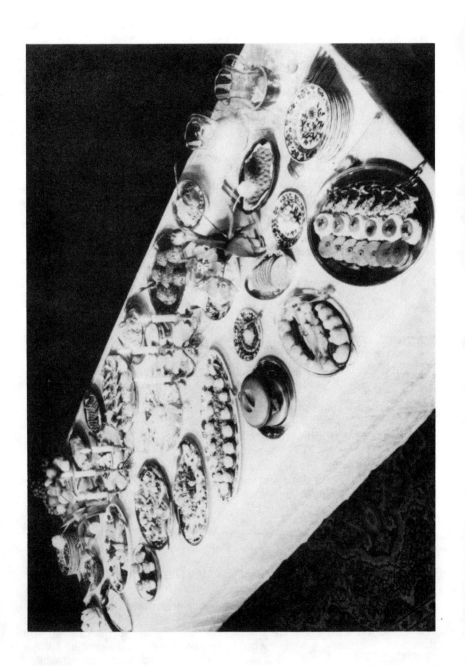

Cold Tidbits
or Snacks

May be served on "Smörgåsbord" or on a tray (one or more different kinds) with cocktail, having buttered crackers or bread, Swedish hard bread, pumpernickel, or any kind preferred.

Pate de Foie Gras

Liver Paste · Chicken Livers

Cauliflower Tidbit

Stuffed Celery No. 1 · Roquefort Snack

Stuffed Celery No. 2 · Liver Roulade

Kielerspraten Naturel · Lobster or Crabmeat

Salmon Patties

Egg Puffles · Egg Anchovy Puffles

Anchovy Snacks

Bird's-Nest *"Fågelbo"*

Cucumber Snacks · Anchovy Balls

Stuffed Whole Celery · Cream Cheese Carrots

Pate de Foie Gras

2 oz. Pate de Foie Gras
1 Philadelphia Cream
   Cheese
2 tbsp. Sherry
Few grains Cayenne
Salt and Pepper to taste

Remove truffle from pate de foie gras and chop fine. Mix cheese, pate de foie gras, cayenne, salt and pepper. Add sherry gradually and work to smooth paste. Make small balls and roll in chopped truffle.

Liver Paste

(Goose, Duck, Chicken or Game)

1 cup Liver
6 Whole Wheat Crackers
1 cup Cream
2 Anchovy Filets
1 tbsp. Flour
2 Eggs
Salt and Pepper

Soak crackers in cream. Carefully remove gall from livers. Wash, scrape and mix livers with other ingredients. Press through a sieve. Butter a plain mould, pour in mixture, and bake in a pan of water about one hour or until a tooth pick inserted in center comes our dry. Chill and serve.

Chicken Livers

1 cup Chicken Livers
½ cup Chopped Gherkins
2 tbsp. Chopped Pickled
   Beets
Mayonnaise
Paprika — Salt — Pepper

Saute chicken livers. Mash to a paste. Add gherkins and seasoning. Moisten with mayonnaise—enough to shape into balls. Roll in beets (squeezed dry).

Cauliflower Tidbit

1 head Cauliflower
Salt
Vinegar
French Dressing

Boil a head of cauliflower in water to which has been added a little salt and a few drops of vinegar. Boil about 20 minutes (not soft). Marinate in French dressing one or two hours. Roll slices of ham, tongue or smoked beef into funnel-like shapes and fill each with one piece of cauliflower.

Stuffed Celery No. 1

1 glass Pineapple Cheese
4 stalks Crisp Celery

Wash celery. Cool in refrigerator until very crisp. Fill with cheese and cut into 1-inch pieces.

Stuffed Celery No. 2

1 pack Philadelphia Cream
    Cheese
½ cup Danish Bleu or
    Rouquefort
Hearts of Celery

Mix cheese and work to a smooth paste. Fill individual stalks of celery hearts, garnish with tiny strips of green pepper, Tomatoes or just with Paprika.
Mix grated any left over cheese add season to taste with cherry, A-1 sauce, cayenne, grated Pineapple etcetera. Whatever you have handy or like.

Roquefort Snacks

¼ lb. Cream Cheese
¼ lb. Roquefort Cheese
1 cup Finely Chopped
    Celery
1 tbsp. Gelatine
½ cup Chopped Walnuts
Pinch of Sugar
Few grains Cayenne
Salt to taste

Mash and mix cheese. Add celery, seasoning, and melted gelatine. Place in refrigerator to harden. With a French vegetable cutter scoop out round balls and roll in walnuts.

Liver Roulade

½ lb. Liverwurst
½ cup Whipped Cream
½ cup Chopped Olives
2 tbsp. Chopped Parsley
Salt — Pepper

Mash liverwurst. Gradually add cream and olives. Salt and pepper to taste. Cool in refrigerator. Shape paste into small forms similar to sausages and roll in chopped parsley.

Kielerspraten Naturel

½ lb. Sprats
1 Lemon

Place sprats on platter. Garnish with slices of lemon and serve very cold with tomatoes or any kind of dainty salad with French dressing.

Lobster or Crabmeat

1 cup Boiled Lobster or
    Crabmeat
½ cup Mayonnaise
1 tbsp. Gelatine
1 tbsp. Chutney
1 Eggwhite
Salt — Pepper
1 tbsp. Chopped Parsley

Cut lobster or crabmeat very fine. Soak gelatine as usual; add to mayonnaise and chutney, and season well, Mix with fish and cool in refrigerator to harden. Shape small portions into any form and roll in parsley.

9

Salmon Patties

½ lb. Smoked Salmon
1 Cream Cheese
1 tbsp. Chopped Dill
Dash of Tabasco
Salt — Pepper

Chop salmon very fine. Mix with cheese and tabasco. Season. Form into small cakes about 1 inch in diameter, and sprinkle with chopped fresh dill.

Egg Puffles

4 Hard-Boiled Eggs
1 tbsp. Escoffier Sauce
Mayonnaise
Salt — Pepper
Parsley (optional)
Puffles

Separate eggs. Mash yolks with escoffier Sauce. Salt and pepper. Soften with mayonnaise so mixture can be squeezed through pastry tube. Shape pyramids on puffles. Sprinkle with chopped eggwhite mixed with parsley (if desired).

Egg Anchovy Puffles

4 Hard-Boiled Eggs
2 tsp. Anchovy Paste
1 cup Mayonnaise
1 tbsp. Chopped Parsley
Puffles

Chop eggs very fine. Mix anchovy paste with mayonnaise, then with eggs. Fill 1 tsp. in each puffle and sprinkle with parsley.

Anchovy Snacks

2 Hard-boiled Eggs
6 Anchovy Filets
2 tbsp. Mayonnaise
3 slices of Bread

Press eggs and anchovies through potato-ricer. Work in mayonnaise. Cut bread in squares or diamond shape. Return mixture to ricer and press over bread. Remove shaped sandwich and garnish with sliced stuffed olives.

Bird's-Nest (Fågelbo)

1 Medium Onion (White)
6 Egg-Yolks
12 Anchovy or Sardellan Filets
½ cup Chopped Pickled Beets
½ cup Chopped Green Peppers
½ cup Chopped Olives
½ cup Chopped Mixed Pickles, Capers, and Parsley
½ cup Chopped Onion
6 slices of Lemon

Cut onion crosswise in half. Remove center of onion. Remove carefully separate layers of onion intact so as to obtain 6 shells or cups. Carefully place 1 raw egg-yolk in each shell, and top with 2 anchovy or sardellan filets crossed. Place filled onion shell on lemon in center of small serving plate. Surround with separate mounds of various chopped ingredients—preferably on small lettuce leaves. Garnish with parsley. (This will make 6 individual portions. It is an unusual and attractive hors d'oeuvre service for a dinner party—the guest using his own discretion combining the various ingredients.) Serve with toast.

Cucumber Snacks

2 Cucumbers
1 cup ground Chicken
1 tbsp. Chili Sauce
½ cup Mayonnaise
Few grains Cayenne
Salt and Pepper

Do not peel cucumbers. Scrape the skin lengthwise with a fork, then cut in ½ inch pieces crosswise and remove the seeds from the centers. Marinate the slices in French Dressing for a couple of hours. Drain and fill with chicken mixed with other ingredients. Garnish and serve cold.

Cream Cheese Carrots

½ lb. Cream Cheese
1 cup grated Carrots
1 tbsp. Gelatin
1 tbsp. Sugar
1 tsp. Paprika
1 tsp. Worcestershire Sauce
2 tbsp. Cream
Few grains Cayenne
Salt and Pepper

Wash and grate unpeeled carrots. Squeeze out most of moisture. Add previously soaked and melted gelatin and seasonings. Add cheese and cream and work to a smooth paste. Chill. With butter paddles shape like tiny carrots, place a sprig of parsley on thin end and arrange on salad platter or serve with cocktail.

Stuffed Whole Celery

2 bunches Celery
1 cup Cream Cheese
½ cup Roquefort Cheese
1 cup chopped Walnuts
1 tbsp. Gelatin
1 tbsp. Sugar
Salt, Pepper & Paprika

Use young crisp celery. Divide and peel each stalk (use potato-peeler, do not scrape) and put in ice water. One hour before serving, drain off water and spread out pieces of celery. Make a filling of the cheese, nuts, gelatin, sugar and spices and fill each stalk with the mixture, starting with inner stalks and adding the larger ones as naturally grown. Press them together, tie and chill. Cut in half-inch slices crosswise. Arrange on a platter, decorate and serve.

Anchovy Balls

6 hard boiled Eggs
1 tbsp. Anchovy Paste
Mayonnaise
Dash of Tabasco
2 tbsp chopped Dill
    or Parsley
1 tbsp. Paprika
4 medium Tomatoes

Cut eggs lengthwise with fluted edged knife. Mash yolks and soften with mayonnaise and anchovy paste; add Tabasco and pinch of sugar. With butter paddles make tiny balls, roll in finely chopped parsley (or dill) mixed with paprika. Place three balls in each egg white and serve on a slice of tomato sprinkled with sugar, salt and pepper.

Hints and Suggestions

Deep Frying

Many of the following recipes for hot tidbits call for deep frying, which is the best method to use in preparing these snacks. In a small household, it is not necessary to have a large iron kettle filled with oil or fat for this purpose. Any small saucepan of a depth sufficient for two or three inches of oil or fat will suffice. It is essential, however, to have a wire basket which fits into the cooking utensil used. (Wire baskets are available in various sizes.)

A good vegetable oil best answers the purpose for deep frying. The odor of animal fat is not only objectionable to many people, but animal fat burns more easily and evaporates quicker than oil.

For deep frying, the temperature of the oil or fat used should be at least 375 to 400 degrees F.; this can be tested by frying a small piece of bread. If the bread turns brown in less than a minute, the oil is hot enough for frying. You will occasionally find that when first immersing the food in the hot fat it does not turn to a rich golden brown. If such is the case, elevate the basket and heat the oil to the right temperature before again immersing the food. This second application should require but several seconds before the food acquires the brown color desired. Cooked ingredients require very little frying whereas food not previously cooked should be immersed in the hot oil for a longer period.

When serving hot tidbits use a glass-skewer or toothpicks.

Hot Tidbit Suggestions
for
Dinner Cocktails

Chicken Liver Tidbit	Fish Tidbit
Chicken Liver and Bacon Tidbit	Herring Filet Tidbit
Liverwurst Tidbit	Oyster Tidbit No. 1
Chicken Tidbit	Oyster Tidbit No. 2
Veal Tidbit	Clam Tidbit
Veal Kidney Tidbit	Kielerspraten Gratin
Mushroom Tidbit	Cheese Tidbit
Anchovies Gratin	Cheese and Walnut Tidbit
Anchovies Fraise	Pastry Tidbits with Fillings
Anchovy Tidbit	Sausage Tidbit
Sardine Tidbit	Roasted Chestnuts

Turkey or Chicken Tidbits

Chicken Liver Tidbit

½ cup Chicken Livers
1 cup Whole Wheat Cracker Crumbs
1 tsp. Escoffier Sauce
1 Egg
½ cup Chopped Olives
Stock or Milk
Oil or Fat

Saute chicken livers in bacon fat or butter. Season well. Mash to a paste. Add chopped olives, egg-yolk, crumbs, and escoffier sauce. Moisten with stock or milk so the mixture can be rolled. Last, fold in eggwhite. Form into small balls and fry in oil or fat. Place a toothpick in each ball and serve very hot.

Chicken Liver and Bacon Tidbit

Chicken Livers
Bacon
Paprika — Salt — Pepper

Divide chicken livers in even pieces ½ x 1 inch. Fold into ½ strip of bacon, and fasten with toothpick. Deep fry, broil or bake.

Liverwurst Tidbit

½ lb. Liverwurst
1 cup White, Soft Bread Crumbs
½ cup Green Chopped Pepper
1 Egg
1 tbsp. or more Catsup or Chilisauce
Salt

Mash liverwurst to a paste. Mix in egg-yolk, green pepper and crumbs. Add enough catsup until mixture is soft enough to roll. Add salt to taste and fold in stiffly beaten eggwhite. Take teaspoonful of mixture and deep fry in oil or fat to a golden brown.

Chicken Tidbit

1 cup Finely Cut Left-Over Chicken
½ cup Chopped Pickles
½ cup Cream Sauce
1 Egg
Cheese Cracker Crumbs
Salt — Pepper

Mix chicken and pickles in cream sauce. Add 1 whole egg and beat well. Season. Make small balls and roll in cheese cracker crumbs. Deep fry.

Veal Tidbit

½ lb. Veal (ground very fine)
2 tbsp. Chili Sauce
½ cup Soft Bread Crumbs
1 Egg
Broth or Milk
Few grains Cayenne
Pinch of Paprika
Salt — Pepper

Mix all ingredients, except eggwhite, to a very smooth dough. Fold in stiffly beaten eggwhite. Place in refrigerator for at least 1 hour preferably longer). Make olive-size balls. Deep fry.

Veal Kidney Tidbit

1 Veal Kidney (Raw—
    ground twice)
1 cup Boiled Rice
1 Egg
1 tbsp. Chopped Olives or
    Pickles
Dash of Cayenne
Salt and Pepper to taste

Mix kidney with hot boiled rice. Add olives or pickles, cayenne, salt and pepper to taste. Add yolk of egg and beat, but do not boil. Fold in stiffly beaten eggwhite. Cool. When ready, take teaspoonful of mixture and deep fry.

Mushroom Tidbit

½ lb. Mushrooms
1 cup White Wine
3 tbsp. Butter
1 tbsp. Flour
Pepper and Salt
Few grains Cayenne
Bacon

Chop mushrooms (not too fine). Simmer in butter five minutes. Sprinkle flour on top, stir, and add wine, cayenne, pepper and salt. Boil slowly until wine is absorbed; cool. Spread on strips of pumpernickel and just before serving, cover top with thin slices of bacon. Brown under broiler and serve hot.

Anchovies Gratin

6 medium potatoes
8 Anchovies
1 tbsp. Anchovy Juice
1 Onion
2 cups Rich milk or Cream
Pepper

Cut raw potatoes in narrow strips. Filet the anchovies and cut into small pieces. Butter a baking dish and place a layer of potatoes, then anchovies, alternating until all is used up, the top layer being of potatoes. Between each layer sprinkle finely chopped onion and a few grains of pepper. Pour milk or cream over all and bake until potatoes are soft and milk has been absorbed.

Anchovies Fraise

10 Anchovies
3 Hard-Boiled Eggs
2 tbsp. chopped Onions
2 tbsp. Chopped Parsley
Few Grains Cayenne
2 tbsp. Butter

Dice hard-boiled eggs (whites and yolks separately). Skin and bone anchovies; cut crosswise. Chop onions and parsley very fine. Mix all ingredients and heat (do not brown) in butter. Serve immediately.

Anchovy Tidbit

2 tsp. Anchovy Paste
    (from tube)
2 cups Mashed Potatoes
1 tsp. Finely Chopped
    Parsley
1 Egg
Dash Tabasco Sauce

Mix ingredients well, except eggwhite which should be beaten stiff and folded in last. Cool. Shape into small balls. Roll in white bread or cracker crumbs and deep fry in oil or fat.

Sardine Tidbit

4 or 5 slices Cracked
    Wheat Bread
2 cans Small Sardines
3 or 4 slices Bacon
2 tbsp. Lemon Juice
Pinch of sugar
Salt — Pepper — Paprika

Pour oil off sardines, carefully empty on dish. Mix lemon juice, sugar, salt and pepper. Marinate and baste the sardines in this for 1 hour. Trim and toast bread light brown. Butter. Cover with sardines, placing strips of bacon on top and broil or bake in hot oven until bacon is crisp. Cut in desirable pieces and serve hot.

Fish Tidbit

½ cup White Wine
½ cup Cream
2 tbsp. Flour
3 tbsp. Butter
Dash of Tabasco
Salt — Pepper
2 Hard-boiled Eggs
1 cup Flaked Salmon
6 small Finger Rolls
1 small can Sardellen

Make a sauce of ingredients; add chopped eggs and flaked salmon and let it come to a boil. Split tiny finger-rolls, remove inside and fill shells with mixture. Top with a few cornflakes and a sardellen spread lengthwise. Heat in a quick oven and serve hot.

Herring Filet Tidbit

½ can "Sill i Dill"
4 Eggs
½ cup Soft White Bread
    Crumbs

Chop 3 hard-boiled eggs fine. Mash "Sill i Dill" to a fine paste, and mix with bread crumbs, then with eggs. Add 1 egg-yolk (raw) and, last, stiffly beaten eggwhite. Drop teaspoonful of mixture in oil to brown.

Oyster Tidbit No. 1

12 Large Oysters
½ cup Oyster Broth
2 tbsp. Butter
1 tbsp. Flour
⅓ cup Cream
Salt — Pepper — Celery
    Salt
Bacon

Boil oysters in own juice one minute. Strain and chop. Melt butter, add flour, broth and seasoning. Cook slowly; add cream; let simmer to a firm consistency. Cool. Spread on nicely shaped canapes; top with a small piece of bacon. Brown under broiler and serve hot.

Oyster Tidbit No. 2

2 dozen Oysters
⅓ cup Butter
⅓ cup Cream
⅓ cup Sherry
½ cup Grapenuts
Dash Cayenne
Salt — Pepper

Saute oysters in butter; add cream, grapenuts, cayenne, salt and pepper to taste. Add sherry. Clean deep oyster shells; place three oysters in each shell. Spread on a layer of mixture and top with a piece of bacon. Brown under broiler and serve hot.

Clam Tidbit

3 dozen small Clams
1 cup Clam Broth
¼ lb. Liver Paste
1 tsp. grated Horseradish
½ cup soft Breadcrumbs
Dash of Tabasco
Pepper and Salt to taste

Let clams come to a boil. Dissolve liver paste in broth. Add other ingredients to same. Clean shells, place four clams in each shell, cover with mixture; sprinkle a few crumbs on top. Broil, and serve hot.

Kielerspraten Gratin

12 Sprats
1 cup Cream
4 Eggs
3 Whole Wheat Crackers
Butter
Salt — Pepper
Few grains Cayenne

Skin and bone sprats. Place filets in buttered baking dish. Beat eggs slightly, add cream, salt, pepper and cayenne. Pour mixture carefully over filets. Sprinkle crackerdust on top and bake until eggs set. Serve hot.

Cheese Tidbit

1 cup Grated Cheese (any kind, or mixed)
1 cup Dry Bread Crumbs— preferably Cracked Wheat
1 tsp. Worcestershire Sauce
½ tsp. Dry Mustard
2 Eggs
Salt and Pepper, if needed

Melt cheese. Add crumbs, Worcestershire Sauce, and mustard. Then add egg-yolks and heat, but do not boil. Fold in stiffly beaten eggwhite. Cool. Take teaspoonful of mixture and deep fry in oil.

Cheese and Walnut Tidbit

½ cup Cracked Crumbs Whole Wheat
1 cup Grated Cheese
1 cup Crushed Walnuts
1 tbsp. A-1 Sauce
1 Egg
1 tsp. Sugar
Few grains Cayenne
Salt — Pepper

Melt cheese. Add crumbs, A-1 sauce, sugar, cayenne, salt and pepper to taste. Mix in walnuts, then add egg-yolks. Heat, but do not boil. Fold in stiffly beaten eggwhite. Take teaspoonful of mixture and deep fry.

Sausage Tidbit

1 lb. Sausage Meat
½ cup Chopped Dill Pickles
2 Eggs
1 tsp. Ground Ginger

Mix all ingredients except eggwhites which should be folded in last. Shape like small sausages and deep fry.

Roasted Chestnuts

1 lb. Chestnuts
½ cup Butter
2 tsp. Lemon Juice
Dash of Tabasco
Salt

Split small end of chestnut crosswise. Place nuts on a layer of rock salt in a heavy frying pan and stir frequently until nuts are soft and shell easily. Serve on a folded napkin. Mix butter with tabasco until soft. Add lemon juice gradually as the butter absorbs it. Cool in refrigerator and scoop out butter balls with a cutter or spoon. Serve with hot chestnuts.

Turkey or Chicken Tidbits

1 cup minced Turkey or
    Chicken
2 tbsp. Butter
1 tbsp. Flour
½ cup light Cream
¼ tsp. Celery Salt
1/3 tsp. Paprika
Dash of Cayenne
1 Egg
Salt and Pepper

Make a cream sauce with butter, flour, cream, and seasoning (or use left-over turkey gravy if available). Add meat and bring to a boil. Add egg yolk and heat but do not boil. Make tiny olive size balls; roll in egg white, then in soft white crumbs and fry. Serve one ball and one stuffed olive on a toothpick.

Pastry Tidbit with Fillings

Roll light pie crust into thin sheets. Cut 2 inch squares (or a little larger if preferred) of pastry and put a teaspoonful of filling on each square. Fold corners over and press together. Brush tops with egg yolks mixed with a little cream. Bake in a medium hot oven until a golden brown Serve hot with cocktails.

Fillings

1. Chop left over chicken, moisten with gravy or cream; add crushed almonds or walnuts. Season to taste.

2. Mix fried or boiled chicken livers with gravy or cream sauce; add two tablespoons of sherry and fill.

3. Cream one cup of cubed shrimps; add one tablespoon capers, salt and pepper to taste.

4. Cream one cup cubed lobster as for Lobster Newburg.

5. To one cup ground ham add 1 teaspoon Worcestershire sauce and 1 tablespoon chopped green pepper.

6. To one cup creamed salmon add one tablespoon chopped dill.

Sauces, Dressings and Relishes

*"Sauces and gravies are the essence of cooking,"
says the chef, and he is right. With a good sauce
or gravy, one may successfully use less expensive
meat or fish, left-overs, etc., and be assured of
producing a very tasty meal.*

*The foundation sauces are — cream sauce, made
of butter, flour, milk or cream, — and brown sauce,
made of drippings from roast (or butter), flour,
stock or water.*

*Different seasonings make different sauces or
gravies, as the following recipes reveal.*

Hollandaise Sauce No. I

Hollandaise Sauce No. 2

Hollandaise Sauce No. 3

French Dressing

Chaufroix Sauce

Swedish Salad Dressing
(Herrgårdssås)

Cucumber Dressing

Sauce Piquante No. I

Sauce Piquante No. 2

Sauce Piquante No. 3

Sharp Sauce (Skarpsås)

Foam Sauce

Cocktail Sauce

Gravlax Sauce

Tartare Sauce

Table Mustard

Lemon Butter Balls

Cucumber Relish

Tomato Relish

Cranberry Relish

Watermelon Rind

Hollandaise Sauce No. 1

3 Egg-yolks
½ cup Butter
½ cup Hot Water or less
1 tbsp. Lemon Juice
Few grains Cayenne
Season to taste

Place egg-yolks in saucepan set in hot water. Add gradually butter, water, and lemon juice. Beat until sauce thickens. Do not boil, as the sauce will separate. Serve at once.

Hollandaise Sauce No. 2

3 Egg-yolks
½ cup Butter
1 tbsp. Flour
½ cup Hot Water or more
1 tbsp. Lemon Juice
Few grains Cayenne
Season to taste

Melt 1 tbsp. flour in part of butter; cook 2 minutes. Then add egg-yolks and other ingredients; proceed as above. (This will not separate as easily, as flour binds the butter and eggs together.) Just before serving, add two stiffly beaten eggwhites.

Hollandaise Sauce No. 3

1 Egg
1 cup Cream Sauce
2 tbsp. Lemon Juice
½ tsp. Sugar
½ cup Mayonnaise

This is a very simply made sauce. To 1 cup cream sauce add 1 egg-yolk, 2 tbsp. lemon juice, ½ tsp. sugar, dash of cayenne, then add slowly ½ cup mayonnaise. Fold in 1 stiffly beaten eggwhite.

French Dressing

¾ cup Olive Oil
1 tsp. Salt
1 tsp. Sugar
¼ tsp. Paprika (optional)
3 tbsp. Vinegar
1 tbsp. Grated Onion
Pinch of Pepper

Shake ingredients together and keep in ice box. One half clove of garlic may be used instead of onion, if desired.

Chaufroix Sauce

½ cup Butter
2 tbsp. Flour
1 cup Strong Chicken or
   Veal Broth (aspic)
1 cup Cream
1 tsp. Celery Salt
1 tsp. Escoffier Sauce
1 tbsp. Sugar
½ cup White Wine
Truffles, Pimento, or Olives

Melt butter. Add flour, broth, cream and seasoning. Cook few minutes. Then add sugar, celery salt, and escoffier sauce. Cut uniform pieces of cold turkey, chicken, or game and place on wire rack. Pour sauce over while warm, and repeat until meat is well covered. Cool. Decorate with truffles, green pepper, pimento, or olives. If strong broth or aspic is not available, add 1 or 2 tsp. of gelatin previously melted.

Swedish Salad Dressing (Herrgårdssås)

3 Eggs
2 tbsp. Olive Oil
1 tbsp. Lemon Juice
1 tbsp. Tarragon Vinegar
1 tbsp. Sugar
1 tbsp. Chopped Dill
1 cup Whipped Cream

Mix two hard boiled egg-yolks with one raw egg-yolk until a smooth paste. Add slowly olive oil, lemon juice, vinegar, sugar, chopped dill, salt and pepper to taste. Fold in one cup whipped cream and add finely chopped eggwhites. Serve with salads, cold fish, or meat.

Cucumber Dressing

1 Cucumber
1 stalk Celery
6 Green Olives
3 small Sweet Pickles
1 tbsp. Tarragon Vinegar
1 tbsp. Lemon Juice
1 tbsp. Chili Sauce
1 cup Whipped Cream

Chop cucumber, celery, olives, and pickles, very fine. Add salt and pepper to taste. To each cup of chopped mixture add 1 tbsp. Tarragon vinegar, 1 tbsp. lemon juice, and 1 tbsp. chili sauce. Fold in one cup whipped cream. Serve with salads, cold fish, or meat. Add sugar if desired.

Sauce Piquant No. 1

½ lb. Butter
1 tbsp. Tarragon Vinegar
1 tbsp. Lemon Juice
2 tbsp. Chopped Olives
2 tbsp. Chopped Pickles
1 tbsp. Sugar
½ tsp. Onion Juice
Few grains Cayenne

Beat butter until light and creamy. Gradually add ingredients. Put in jar. Keep in ice box. Serve with fish or cold meat.

Sauce Piquant No. 2

½ cup Butter
½ cup Grated Cheese
1 tbsp. Brown Sugar
4 Gingersnaps (Soaked in
    1 cup water)
4 tbsp. White Vinegar
1 med. Sliced Lemon
2 Bay Leaves
½ cup Seedless Raisins,
    chopped
10 chopped Blanched
    Almonds

Melt butter and cheese. Add all ingredients except raisins and almonds, and cook slowly for 15 minutes. Strain. Last, mix in raisins and chopped almonds. Used with fish, cold meat or salads.

Sauce Piquant No. 3

4 hard-boiled Eggs
1 tsp. French Mustard
1 cup Olive Oil
½ cup White Vinegar
Juice and Rind of Lemon
1 tbsp. Sugar
2 tbsp. mixed Pickles
1 tbsp. Chopped Dill
1 tbsp. finely cut Chives
Salt — Pepper

Press egg yolks through a sieve and gradually work in other ingredients. Add pickles, dill and chives, salt and pepper to taste. Cut egg whites in narrow strips and fold in. If sauce is too heavy add a little vinegar or water. Serve with cold meat or fish.

Sharp Sauce (Skarpsås)

1 cup Bordelaise Vinegar
1 tbsp. Lemon Juice
½ cup Sugar (less, if desired)
1 tbsp. Onion Juice
1 tbsp. Dry Mustard
Few grains Cayenne
Dash of Tabasco Sauce
2 tbsp. Chopped Fresh Dill

Shake all ingredients together. Salt and pepper to taste. Keep in cold place and use for cold fish and meats.

Foam Sauce

1 cup Cream Sauce
¼ cup Chili Sauce or Italian Tomato Paste
1 tbsp. Sugar
2 Eggs

To 1 cup of cream sauce, add ¼ cup of chili sauce, or Italian tomato paste, (not too hot) and 1 tbsp. sugar. Boil two or three minutes and remove from fire. Then add 2 egg-yolks; heat, but do not boil. Fold in 2 stiffly beaten eggwhites and serve hot.

Cocktail Sauce

1 cup Chopped Celery
1 tbsp. Chopped Chives
1 cup Tomato Ketchup
½ tsp. Dry Mustard
2 tbsp. Vinegar
1 tsp. Salt
¼ tsp. Pepper
1 tbsp. Grated Horseradish

Mix ingredients together and keep in icebox. Serve with cold shrimp, crabmeat, oysters, etc.

Gravlax - Sauce

2½ tbsp. English Mustard prepared
5 tbsp. gran. Sugar
½ tsp. Salt
2 tbsp. Olive Oil
1 tbsp. (or more) Vinegar
1 tbsp. Heavy Cream
2 tbsp. Chopped Dill

Mix mustard, sugar and salt add slowly oil and vinegar, then cream and last dill, serve cold.

Tartare Sauce

Mayonnaise
½ cup each of finely chopped Dill Pickles, Mixed Pickles, Celery, Green Pepper, hard fresh Tomatoes.
2 tbsp. Pimentoes
2 tbsp. Parsley
2 tbsp. Sugar
Juice of 2 Lemons
Salt — Pepper

Combine all ingredients and mix in enough Mayonnaise to spread. Keep in refrigerator and serve with hot or cold fish, cold meats, sandwiches, etc.

Table Mustard

1 Egg
1 heaping tbsp. Dry Mustard
1 tbsp. Sugar
3 tbsp. Tarragon Vinegar
Pinch of Salt
Few grains Cayenne

Beat egg thoroughly, and mix with ingredients well. Let thicken in double boiler, stirring constantly. Put in jar and keep in ice box.

Lemon Butter Balls

1 cup Butter
2 tbsp. Lemon Juice
1 tsp. grated Lemon Rind
1 tsp. Finely Chopped Parsley
1 tsp. Sugar
Few grains Cayenne
Dash of Tabasco
Salt to taste

Work butter until light and creamy. Add ingredients—except parsley. Let harden in icebox. Make tiny balls with butter paddles. Roll in parsley. Arrange pyramid-shaped on glass dish. Serve with fried fish.

Cucumber Relish

6 large Cucumbers
1 cup Vinegar
½ cup Water
1 tbsp. Mixed Spices
1 stick Cinnamon
1 piece Ginger
1½ cup Sugar

Peel and cut cucumbers lengthwise. Remove seeds, cut crosswise in half-inch thicknesses (use a fluted knife) and soak for a few hours in two quarts of water, to which has been added one tbsp. salt. Drain. Mix vinegar, water, sugar and spices and boil cucumbers 20 to 30 minutes. Cool. Keep in refrigerator and serve with roasts, ragouts, minced meats, etc.

Cranberry Relish

2 qts. Cranberries
3 Seedless Oranges
1 lb. or more Sugar
1 tsp. Salt

Grind berries and oranges through a food chopper; add sugar and salt, stirring evenly ten to fifteen minutes. Serve raw.

Tomato Relish

10 lbs. Tomatoes (not too
    ripe)
2 tbsp. mixed Spices
2 Lemons
1 tbsp. grated Horseradish
2 cups Maple Syrup
2 tbsp. Salt

Plunge tomatoes in boiling water 1 minute. Peel, cut and boil in stewing kettle 20 minutes. Set aside, and when settled, pour off some of the juice. Quarter lemons lengthwise and slice very thin. Add to tomatoes with spices, horseradish and salt. Simmer slowly 30 minutes. Add syrup and cook 10 minutes longer. Keep in refrigerator and serve with hot or cold fish, meat, snacks, etc.

Watermelon Rind

1 Watermelon
2 cups White Wine
2 cups Vinegar
2 cups Water
1 stick Cinnamon
2 tbsp. Mixed Spices
2 lb. Sugar

Split melon and use inside for fruit cup salad or anything you choose but remove the red part and seeds. Peel the skin of cut lengthwise inch and a half, cut crossways in desirable pieces "with fluted cutter" soak in water with a tbsp. salt to each quart for few hours. Strain. Boil in wine, vinegar, water with spices about 45 min. or till melon is reasonably soft. Insted of sugar one may use maplesugar or part honey if desired.

Hints or Suggestions

There are any number of good Mayonnaise Dressings, Salad Dressings, and Russian Dressings on the market, which can be bought already prepared and less expensive than to make. To these any seasonings may be added. If a very light and fluffy sauce is desired, fold in whipped cream or stiffly beaten egg whites.

Fish Food

When preparing a fish dinner with baked or boiled fish, take the trouble to boil the head, tail, and bones with 1 bay leaf, a few allspice, salt, pepper and celery salt. Strain and use the broth to boil or baste the fish; it wil enrich the dish considerably. The best flavored part of the fish is the head. A couple of fish-heads make an excellent meal of creamed fish, gratin, or chowder.

If boiled fish with cream sauce is served, steam fish in milk instead of water, and use same broth for sauce.

The best bread crumbs are made from white bread one to two days old. Rub through a colander or a grater.

Pickled Herring "Inlagd Sill"
Glasmästaresill
Salt Herring with Onion Sauce
    "Stekt Sill Scandia"
Herring Roe
Fresh Herring
Herring Gratin No. 1 "Sill Gratin"
Herring Gratin No. 2 "Sill Gratin"
Herring in Paper "Sill i Papper"
Herring and Egg Saute
Broiled Herring
Parsley Herring
Herring Salad "Sill Salad"
Fried Fresh Sardines
    "Stekt Strömming"
Fresh Sardines with Anchovies
Fresh Sardines with Tomatoes
Fresh Sardine Flounders
Sardines with Eggs and Anchovies
Sardine Souffle
Marinated Sardines "Gravad
    Strömming"
"Lite Men Gott"
Boiled Rullmops
Baked Rullmops
Creamed Oysters
Creamed Oysters with Mushrooms
Oyster Croquette
Oysters and Calf Brains
Oysters au Gratin
Oysters in Marinade
Mussels
Mussels au Gratin
Mussels Marinade
Mussels Mariniere
Frogs Legs
Crabmeat Gratin
Plain Boiled Shrimps

Crabmeat Newburg
Hard-Shell Crabs
Cold Boiled Lobster
Lobster Newburg
Broiled Lobster
Lobster Croquettes
Lobster Thermidor
Crawfish "Kräftor"
Crawfish Thermidor
Baked Eel "Ungstekt Ål"
Pickled Eel "Inkokt Ål"
Boiled Pike "Kokt Gädda
    med Smör Pepparrot"
Pickled Pike "Inkokt Gädda"
Fish Croquettes
Boiled Halibut with Shrimp Sauce
Halibut Gratin
Fish Gratin No. 1
Fish Gratin No. 2
Anchovies Gratin
Steamed Filet of Perch-
    Swedish Style
Baked Mackerel
Boiled Salmon
Salmon Pudding No. 1
Salmon Pudding No. 2
Smoked Salmon with Eggs and
    Spinach
Pickled Salmon
Whole Salmon with Mayonnaise
Marinated Salmon "Gravlax"
Salmon and Macaroni Pudding
Codfish Gratin
Baked Cod, Bass or Haddock
    with Oysters
Creamed Finnan Haddie

Shrimps a la Newburg

Mock Turtle Stew

Pickled Herring (Inlagd Sill)

3 Iceland Herring
1 cup White Vinegar (or more)
½ cup Granulated Sugar
½ cup Finely Chopped Onions
3 Bay Leaves
12 Whole Allspice
Pepper

Select the best large salt herring. Soak in cold water over night. Split, skin and remove all bones. Cut in tiny strips crosswise. Slide knife under the cut filet and place in china or glass dish. Mix ingredients and pour over herring. Let stand several hours before serving. If available, add 2 or 3 sprays of fresh dill.

Glasmästaresill

6 Herrings salt
3 cups Vinegar
3 cups Water
1 cup each of sliced Carrots, Turnips, Onions and Celery
½ Cup Leeks
½ Cup Fresh Dill
1 tbsp. Crushed Allspice
1 Cup Sugar
Salt and Pepper to taste

Clean and soak Herring over night. Mix Vinegar, Water and all ingredients, stir till sugar melts and pour over Herring placed in a deep crock. After 5 days it should be ready.

Salt Herring with Onion Sauce (Stekt Sill Scandia)

2 Salt Herrings
1 cup Sliced Onions
½ cup Butter or Fat
1 tbsp. Flour
½ tsp. Sugar
2 cups Milk
½ tps. Paprika
1 Egg
⅔ cup Bread Crumbs
¼ tsp. White Pepper

Soak and clean 2 herrings, as in Pickled Herring. Bone, cut each filet in half. Dip in beaten egg and roll in bread crumbs. Fry in hot pork fat or butter until golden brown. Place filets on hot serving platter. Simmer onions in same pan; add flour, milk, sugar, paprika, and pepper. Boil until mixture thickens. Pour this sauce around fish. Serve with plain boiled potatoes.

Fresh Herring

6 Fresh Herrings
½ cup Flour
½ cup Bread Crumbs
1 Egg or more
⅓ cup Sugar
1 cup Vinegar
½ cup Onions
4 Bay Leaves
12 Allspice
Salt and Pepper

Clean, wash, and dry on towel. Make three incisions on each side with sharp knife—keep fish whole. Dip in flour, then in egg; last, dip in bread crumbs mixed with salt and pepper. Fry in hot fat or butter. Serve with boiled potatoes. If served cold, pour over a cup of white vinegar mixed with sugar; cover with sliced onions, bay leaves, and whole allspice.

Herring Gratin No. 1 (Sill Gratin)

2 Large Salt Herrings
6 Raw Potatoes, medium size
1 cup Sliced Onions
Bread Crumbs
Butter

Soak and clean herring, as in Pickled Herring. Place in buttered baking dish a layer of sliced potatoes; season; then add a layer of herring cut in 1-inch slices. Cover with sliced onion; pepper, and repeat layers, finishing with potatoes. Sprinkle top with bread crumbs and a generous amount of butter. Bake in moderate oven about 45 minutes.

Herring Gratin No. 2 (Sill Gratin)

2 Large Herrings
6 Cold-Boiled Potatoes
3 Eggs
2 cups Milk
1 tsp. Sugar
1 tsp. Parsley
Salt — Pepper

Proceed as in Herring Gratin No. 1, using thin layers of boiled potatoes in place of raw. Pour over a custard made of eggs, milk, sugar, parsley, salt and pepper. Bake in a moderate oven 30 minutes.

Herring in Paper (Sill i Papper)

4 Herrings, medium size
1½ cups Sliced Boiled Potatoes
1 cup Sliced Onions
2 tbsp. Chopped Parsley
Butter-Fat
Pepper

Soak herring 10 hours. Cut head and tail off. Split fish in back and remove bones, but leave stomach whole. Fill with potatoes, sauted, onions, and parsley. Cut a round piece of white or brown wrapping paper from 10 to 12 inches in diameter, and fold in half. Place herring on generous amount of butter inside. Start folding edges of paper from one end by overlapping edge 1-inch at a time, which will make package tight. Fry in fat and place in warm oven few minutes. If preferred, one may omit potatoes in herring and serve creamed potatoes instead.

Herring and Egg Saute

2 Herrings
4 Hard-boiled Eggs
1 cup Chopped Onions
½ cup Cream
1 tbsp. Chopped Dill or Parsley
⅓ cup Butter
Dash of Pepper
Salt if necessary

Soak whole herrings over night. Clean, skin, and remove all bones. Cut herrings in small squares. Chop hard-boiled eggs (not too fine). Simmer chopped onions in butter until soft but not brown; add herring, cook one minute. Add eggs and cream; heat well. Add seasoning and sprinkle dill or parsley over. Serve hot.

Broiled Herring

2 Salt Herrings, large
1 cup Cream
1 tbsp. Chopped Chives
Salad Oil
Pepper

Soak, split and bone herring. Place in salad oil half hour. Put two halves together like whole. Place in broiler and brown on both sides—then put in baking dish and pour cream over. Sprinkle with black pepper and chives. When cream is partly absorbed, serve hot with plain boiled potatoes.

Parsley Herring

4 Holland Salt Herrings
1 cup Butter
1 cup Chopped Parsley
Juice of 1 Lemon
Pepper

Soak, split and bone herring. Mix other ingredients together. Let come to a boil. Heat a serving platter. Place filets on platter and pour over mixture. Serve *immediately*.

Herring Salad (Sill Salad)

2 large Salt Herrings
1 cup Cooked Veal
1 cup Potatoes
1 cup Boiled Beets
1 cup Apples
½ cup Onions
½ cup Pickles
1 cup French Dressing
½ cup White Vinegar
1 tbsp. Sugar
1 or 2 Eggs (Hard-Boiled)

Soak herring over night. Clean, skin, bone, and cube. Mix with chopped veal, potatoes, beets, apples, onions, and pickles. Add French dressing and vinegar (and 1 cup mayonnaise, if preferred). Heap on platter and decorate with sliced or quartered hard-boiled eggs, parsley and mayonnaise.

Herring Roe

1 can Herring Roe
½ cup Butter or Fat

Fry in butter or pork fat. Season well and serve hot.

Fried Fresh Sardines (Stekt Strömming)

2 lbs. Fresh Sardines
1 Egg
Flour
Salt
Pepper
2 cups Bread Crumbs
Fat or Butter

Clean and wipe sardines with damp cloth. Dip sardines in flour mixed with salt and pepper, then in eggs, and last in crumbs. Fry in butter, or deep fat.

Fresh Sardines with Anchovies

1 lb. Sardines (Fresh)
Anchovies
Bread Crumbs
⅓ cup Butter
Pepper
Salt

Clean sardines. Place inside each sardine 1 anchovy filet. Arrange layers in buttered baking dish. Season. Sprinkle buttered bread crumbs on top and bake from 15 to 20 minutes or dip in egg and crumbs and fry in butter.

Fresh Sardines with Tomatoes

12 or more Fresh Sardines
(medium size)
3 tbsp. Butter
1 tbsp. Chopped Onions
3 medium sized Tomatoes
1 tsp. Sugar
1 tbsp. Chopped Parsley
1 tbsp. soft Bread Crumbs
Salt and Pepper

Clean, split and bone fish and lay on a towel. Dry and sprinkle with salt and pepper. Put halves together and place in buttered baking dish. Sprinkle with onions and parsley and cover with sliced tomatoes. Sprinkle with sugar, salt and pepper and cover with bread crumbs. Bake 30 minutes and serve hot in same dish.

Sardine Flounders

2 doz. fresh Sardines
(even size)
½ cup Butter
½ chopped Parsley
1 tsp Anjovie Paste
1 Egg
1 Bread Crumbs
Salt — Pepper

Clean and bone Sardines but leave skin whole in back. Soften butter add parsley and anjoviepaste. Spread one flaket fllet with mixture and cover with another filet. Dip filet in flour, egg and crumbs fry in butter and serve hot. Omit anjoviepaste and season with salt and pepper if preferred.

Sardines with Eggs and Anchovies

1 box Large Sardines (skinless and boneless)
Tube of Anchovy Paste
3 Eggs
1 cup Rich Milk
Butter
Few grains Cayenne

Butter a baking dish. Carefully split sardines. Place in dish, spreading a thin layer of anchovy paste on each half. Mix milk and eggs together, pouring carefully over sardines, so that they will stay in place. Bake in a moderate oven until eggs are set. Serve hot.

Sardine Souffle

1 can Large Sardines
1 cup Cream Sauce
3 Egg Yolks
1 tsp. Chopped Italian
Pepper
Salt
3 Egg Whites

Mash sardines through a sieve or colander. Mix with cream sauce and egg yolks. Add finely chopped Italian pepper and salt to taste. Fold in stiffly beaten egg whites, and pour in well buttered baking dish. Bake 15 minutes and serve immediately.

Marinated Sardines (Gravad Strömming)

2 lbs. Sardines (Fresh)
1 cup Vinegar
2 tbsp. Sugar
3 tbsp. Olive Oil
1 tbsp. Chopped Dill
1 tsp. Dry Mustard
Salt
Pepper

Clean, split, skin, and bone sardines. Make dressing of other ingredients. Pour dressing over filets and let stand in icebox for a few hours before serving.

"Lite Men Gott"

Filets of Anchovies or
   "Sill i Dill"
Raw shoe-string Potatoes

Cover the bottom of a buttered baking dish with filets of anchovies or "Sill i Dill", then add a layer (about 1½ inches) of raw shoe-string potatoes and dot top generously with butter. Bake in oven about 20 to 30 minutes and serve hot in same dish.

Boiled Rullmops

2 lbs. Fresh Sardines
3 Bay Leaves
10 Whole Allspice
1 Lemon
Salt
Pepper
Paprika
Chopped Parsley

Clean and bone fresh sardines, leaving the back whole. Sprinkle with salt, pepper and paprika, also chopped parsley. Roll sardines from head down. Place in a shallow buttered dish. Boil bay leaves, whole allspice, slices of lemon, salt and pepper to taste, with bones (in enough water to cover) 15 minutes. Pour over fish and steam for 10 to 15 minutes (until soft). Serve hot or cold.

Baked Rullmops

Prepare as Boiled Rullmops. Instead of steaming, place in buttered baking dish. Sprinkle with buttered crumbs and bake in hot oven from 10 to 15 minutes. Serve hot. Smelts may be prepared in the same manner.

Creamed Oysters

2 doz. Large Oysters
½ cup Cream
4 tbsp. Butter
1 tbsp. Flour
Salt and Pepper
"3 tbsp. White Wine"

Boil oysters 1 minute. Strain. Make sauce using part oyster broth and part cream. Season well. Pour over oysters and serve hot. This may also be placed in baking dish and covered with grated cheese or bread crumbs and baked. White wine may be added if desired.

Creamed Oysters with Mushrooms

4 doz. Oysters
½ lb. Mushrooms
3 tbsp. Butter
1 wineglass Sherry
½ cup Cream
1 tbsp. Flour
Tabasco or Cayenne
Salt and Pepper

Place oysters in saucepan and let come to a boil. Remove oysters, and boil oyster juice down to 1 cup. Saute button mushroom caps in 3 tbsp. butter, and sprinkle over a scant tbsp. flour. Add oyster broth and ½ cup cream. Season with a pinch of sugar, salt, pepper, a dash of tabasco or a few grains cayenne, and sherry wine.

Oyster Croquette

2 doz. Oysters (Large)
1 cup Cracker Crumbs
2 Eggs
1 tbsp. Chutney
Salt and Pepper

Boil oysters in liquid one minute. Remove and cube. Make thick sauce of oyster liquid, using cracker crumbs for thickening instead of flour. Add 2 egg-yolks, 1 tbsp. chutney sauce, salt and pepper. Add oyster cubes. Cool and shape in cones. Dip in flour, then in eggwhites and last in crumbs. Deep fry and serve hot with or without lobster, shrimp, or tomato sauce.

Oysters and Calf Brains

2 Calf Brains
2 doz. Oysters
1 tsp. Lemon Juice
1 tsp. Soy (Fuji Sauce)
Salt and Pepper
Cream

Place calf brains in cold water and let stand 30 minutes. Remove skin and blood cells (if any). Boil oysters 2 minutes. Remove oysters and boil calf brains in oyster broth 10 to 15 minutes. Make sauce of oyster broth and cream. Season well. Add lemon juice and Soy. Add oysters to sauce and pour over hot calf brains.

Oysters au Gratin

3 doz. Oysters (on deep half
    of shell)
2 cups Oyster Juice
2 tbsp. Butter
1 tbsp. Flour
1 tsp. Worcestershire Sauce
1 tsp. Lemon Juice
¼ tsp. Celery Salt
¼ tsp. Paprika
Salt and Pepper
4 oz. Pate de Foie Gras,
    Liver Paste or Liver-
    wurst.

Make a sauce of butter, flour and seasonings. Last work in the liver paste. Cover each oyster with sauce and place shells on a bed of rocksalt in a roasting pan. Bake 2 or 3 minutes in a very hot oven and serve immediately, or broil.

Oysters in Marinade

1 qt. Large Oysters
1 yellow Onion sliced thin
3 Bay leaves
6 Whole Allspice
6 Whole Black Peppers
¼ tsp. Mustard Seed
1 thinly sliced Lemon
1 cup Oyster Broth
½ cup Vinegar
Salt to taste

Boil oysters in liquid. Strain. Boil down broth to one cup and chill. Mix all ingredients with broth, pour over oysters and let stand one hour or more. Serve.

Mussels

10 doz. Mussels
2 cups Water
1 cup White Wine
1 medium sized Onion, minced
1 tbsp. chopped Parsley
1 Bay Leaf
6 Allspice
Pinch of black pepper
Salt if necessary

Clean and brush mussels well. Boil all other ingredients in a large kettle a few minutes. Put in mussels, cover tight and boil 2 or 3 minutes. As the mussels open, pick them out, separate shell over kettle (to save broth) and leave mussel on one-half of shell, discarding the other half. Place on hot serving platter or in deep bowl. Strain the broth over or serve separately. (If too much liquid, boil it down to about 2 cups).

Mussels au Gratin

50 Mussels
2 tbsp. Butter
1 tbsp. Flour
1 Cup Musselbroth
1 tsp. Worcestersauce
1 tbsp. Lemonjuice
2 Eggs
Salt and Pepper to taste

Prepare mussels as in preceding recipe. Take them out of shells and place in buttered baking dish. Melt 2 tablespoons butter with 1 tablespoon flour, 1 cup mussel broth, 1 teaspoon Worcestershire Sause, juice of half a lemon, salt and pepper to taste. After partly cooling, stir in 2 egg yolks and last, 2 stiffly beaten egg whites. Pour over mussels in dish and bake in moderate oven 10 to 15 minutes. Serve immediately.

Mussels in Marinade

Prepare mussels as No. 1 recipe. When cool, add to one cup of musselbroth 2 tablespoons olive oil, 1 tablespoon lemon juice, pinch of sugar, 1 teaspoon chopped green dill. Leave mussels in marinade one hour or more before serving.

Mussels Mariniere

10 doz. Mussels
½ pt. White Wine
½ cup Chopped Onions
1 stalk Celery (whole)
Salt and Pepper
1 cup Hollandaise Sauce

Brush and clean mussels very well and put them in a large kettle with celery, onions, salt and pepper. Cover and steam mussels. When they open, discard one shell, leaving mussel on one and place in a chafing-dish or casserole and cover. Pour liquid from large kettle slowly into a sauce pan, leaving any possible sand in bottom. Briskly stir in the Hollandaise Sauce. Heat, (do not boil), pour over mussels and serve very hot.

Frogs Legs

1 lb. Frogs Legs
Butter
1 cup Sliced Mushrooms
1 tbsp. Flour
1 cup Broth or Milk
4 tbsp. Sherry or White Wine
1 cup Cream
Salt — Pepper — Paprika

Wash and dry frogs legs. Dip in flour mixed with salt, pepper, and paprika. Fry in butter until golden brown. Lower flame and add 1 cup broth or milk. Let simmer until tender. Make sauce of 2 tbsp. butter, 1 tbsp. flour, 1 cup cream. Add 4 tbsp. sherry or white wine, 1 cup sliced mushrooms previously sauted in butter. Pour sauce around frogs' legs on platter.

Crabmeat au Gratin

3 cups Fresh Crabmeat (or 1 lb. Canned)
2 cups Rich Cream Sauce
Grated Cheese
Bread Crumbs
Dash of Tabasco
Salt — Pepper

Mix crabmeat with cream sauce; add seasoning. Place in buttered baking dish. Sprinkle with cheese and bread crumbs. Brown in oven or under broiler.

Crabmeat Newburg

1 lb. Canned Crabmeat
2 cups Cream and Milk (Mixed)
2 Egg-yolks
1 glass Sherry (wineglass)
2 tbsp. Brandy
Butter
Few grains Cayenne
Salt — Pepper

Heat crabmeat in butter. Season with salt, pepper, and cayenne. Stir in cream and bring to a boil. Thicken with egg-yolks which have been diluted in 2 tbsp. cream and brandy. Add sherry, but do not boil. Serve with toast.

Hard-Shell Crabs

12 Hard-Shell Crabs
1 cup Salt
Few sprigs Fresh or Dry Dill
½ cup Olive Oil
½ cup Vinegar
1 tsp. Dry Mustard
1 tbsp. Sugar
1 tbsp. Chopped Fresh Dill
Salt — Pepper

Wash crabs in cold salted water. Plunge in boiling water (about 1 gallon) to which 1 cup salt and dill have been added. Boil from 20 to 40 minutes, according to size of crabs. Cool in same water. For sauce mix mustard, sugar, vinegar, oil, salt and pepper, and finely chopped dill. Serve crabs cold with sauce.

Cold Boiled Lobster

Live Lobsters (med. size)
1 cup Salt
Few sprays Fresh or Dry Dill
1 Lemon

Plunge live lobsters into briskly boiling water. Use 1 cup salt to each gallon of water, and add the dill. Boil from 15 to 25 minutes, depending on size. Let cool in same water. Split and remove intestinal vein, also gall. Crack claws. Serve with mayonnaise or sharp sauce. Garnish with fresh dill and lemon.

Lobster Newburg

3 cups Boiled Lobster (cubed)
1 cup Cream
3 Egg-yolks
1 glass Sherry
2 tbsp. Brandy
Few grains Cayenne
Salt — Pepper

Saute cubed lobsters in butter for about 2 minutes. Season with salt, pepper, and cayenne. Moisten with half of sherry. Stir in cream, and bring to a boil. Thicken with egg-yolks which have been beaten with 2 tbsp. cream and 2 tbsp. brandy. Stir well until it thickens, but do not boil. Add remainder of sherry, and serve on toast.

Broiled Lobster

2 Lobsters (not less than 2 lbs. each)
Butter
2 tbsp. Lemon Juice
Dash of Tabasco
Salt — Pepper — Paprika

Clean and split live lobsters, removing gall and intestinal vein. Broil under hot flame. (Slow broiling makes lobster tough.) Melt butter; add lemon juice and seasoning. Pour over lobster and serve very hot.

Lobster Croquettes

2 cups of Boiled or Canned
fresh Lobster
½ lb. Mushrooms
1 cup Cream Sauce
2 Eggs
1 tbsp. Chutney
Flour and Crumbs
Salt — Pepper

Dice lobster. Saute chopped mushrooms. Add to cream sauce and let come to a boil. Add egg-yolks, chutney, salt and pepper. Let thicken but do not boil. Cool and shape into cones or balls. Dip in flour, then in beaten eggwhites, and last in the crumbs. Deep fry. Serve with tomato or Piquant Sauce.

Lobster Thermidor

2 Boiled Lobsters
½ lb. Fresh Mushrooms
1 cup Cream Sauce
2 Egg-yolks
Few grains Cayenne
Dash of Tabasco
Bread Crumbs
Salt — Pepper — Paprika

Split boiled lobsters. Remove meat and clean shells thoroughly. Cube lobster meat and mix with cream sauce. Add egg-yolks and other ingredients, including sauted mushrooms. Fill shells with mixture and cover with buttered bread crumbs. Brown slightly in a very hot oven or under broiler.

Crawfish (Kräftor)

30 - 40 Crawfish
1 cup Salt
Few sprigs Fresh or Dry
Dill

It is most important that all crawfish are alive. Wash in cold water. (To thoroughly cleanse, let crawfish remain in cold water, to which 1 cup salt has been added, from 15 to 20 minutes. Pick over again to be sure that all are alive.) Plunge into boiling water (about 1 gallon) to which 1 cup salt and dill have been added. Cook for 15 minutes after water again comes to a boil. Let cool in same water. Serve ice cold. Garnish with fresh sprigs of dill.

Crawfish Thermidor

Carefully remove the shell with head and keep whole. Remove meat from tails, cube very fine, prepare like lobster thermidor, omitting mushrooms, stuff the small shells dust with crumbs and brown under broiler.

Baked Eel (Ugnstekt Ål)

1 Eel, weighing 2 to 2½ lbs.
Butter
Lemon
Worcestershire Sauce
1 tsp. Dry Mustard

Skin, split and bone eel. Spread a mixture of butter, salt, pepper, a few drops of lemon juice, dry mustard, and a dash of Worcestershire sauce on each half. Sprinkle with fine buttered bread crumbs and bake in moderate oven 30 to 40 minutes. Garnish with slices of lemon. Serve hot or cold with a sharp sauce (Skarpsas).

Pickled Eel (Inkokt Ål)

1 Eel, weighing about 2 lbs.
Lemon
Bay Leaves
Allspice
Celery Salt
Dill
1 tsp. Gelatin

Skin and clean eel. Cut on bias in 1-inch pieces. Boil slowly in enough water to cover. Add a few slices of lemon, 2 or 3 bay leaves, a few whole allspice, pinch celery salt, fresh or dry dill and salt and pepper to taste. Cook until eel is very soft. If there is too much broth remove eel and boil down to get it strong and tasty. If molded shape is preferred, add 1 tbsp. melted gelatin to broth; strain over fish; cool and let set. Turn out on dish. Decorate with fresh dill.

Boiled Pike (Kokt Gädda med Smör och Pepparrot)

2 lbs. Pike
2 Bay Leaves
1 Lemon
1 cup Butter
½ cup Fresh Horseradish (grated)

Clean fish and boil slowly in water, sufficient to cover, with salt, pepper, and 2 bay leaves. Cook about 30 minutes and serve on napkin covered platter. Garnish with lemon and parsley. Instead of sauce serve melted butter and grated fresh horseradish on separate dishes or heat butter with horseradish.

Pickled Pike (Inkokt Gädda)

2 lbs. Pike
2 Bay Leaf
½ tsp. Celery Salt
8 Allspice

Clean, split and bone fish. Boil bones, head and tail in water with salt, pepper, celery salt, 1 bay leaf and whole allspice for 30 minutes. Cut fish in 1-inch pieces crossways. Strain fish broth over and boil slowly until soft (about 30 minutes). Serve cold, decorate with fresh dill.

Fish Croquettes

1½ cups left-over Fish
1½ cups Cream Sauce
2 Eggs
Parsley

Mix fish with rich cream sauce. Add egg-yolks. Heat but do not boil. Season well. Cool. Shape into cones. Dip in flour, then in white of eggs, and again in flour. Cook in deep fat. Serve with large sprays of parsley which also have been cooked in deep fat until crisp, about one-half a minute. Mound parsley in center of platter, arrange the croquettes around. Fish croquettes may also be served with cream sauce seasoned with anchovy paste, tomato, or chutney.

Boiled Halibut with Shrimp Sauce

4 lb. Halibut
2 cups Milk
1 cup White Wine
1 Bayleaf
6 Allspice
1 Lemon
1 tbsp. Sugar
1 tbsp. Salt
¼ tsp. Pepper
Butter
18 Boiled Shrimps

Select a chicken halibut weighing about 4 pounds. Cut 2 filets from each side, starting from middle and sliding knife to edge. Put skin side down and cut fish from skin. Boil bones and skin with spices in milk for about 15 minutes. Strain. Butter an oblong baking dish. Place filets in dish and pour broth over. Cover with waxpaper and boil in oven 15 to 20 minutes; add wine and cook 3 to 5 minutes longer. Garnish with shelled hot shrimps and serve in same dish.

Halibut Gratin

2 lbs. Halibut
½ lb. Crabmeat
12 Clams
1 Can Tomatoes
1 medium Onion
½ clove Garlic (if desired)
1 tbsp. Sugar
1 Bay Leaf
6 Allspice
Juice of 1 Lemon
Salt and Pepper

Skin and bone fish. Place in buttered baking dish. Boil fish bones and clam juice with remaining ingredients for 15 minutes. Season to taste. Strain over fish and bake in moderate oven 15 to 30 minutes. Then cover with clams and crabmeat and bake a few minutes more. Serve hot from baking dish.

Fish Gratin No. 1

Left-over Fish
Cream Sauce
Fish Broth
Grated Cheese
Bread Crumbs

Use any left-over fish, or purchase fish heads (the head being the most savory part of the fish). Boil with the usual seasonings in a small amount of water. Pick meat from bones and mix with a thick sauce made of part fish broth and part cream. Season well. Fill in buttered baking dish. Sprinkle with grated cheese or buttered bread crumbs. Bake in oven 20 minutes.

Note: For richness add egg-yolks to sauce and fold in beaten white.

Fish Gratin No. 2

2 cups Boiled Fish
1 cup Shrimp or Lobster
1 cup White Wine
1 tbsp. Grated Onions
1 tsp. Chopped Chives or
    Leek
Butter — Salt — Pepper

Place pieces of fish and shrimp or lobster in well buttered baking dish. Saute onions and chives in 2 tbsp. butter for 2 minutes. Add salt and pepper to taste. Add wine and heat. Pour over fish; dot with butter and bake in hot oven a few minutes. Serve hot.

Anchovies au Gratin

1 can Skinned and Bone-
    less Anchovies
3 Eggs
1 pt. Rich Milk
1 tbsp. Chopped Parsley

Place anchovies in a buttered baking dish. Mix together eggs, milk, and chopped parsley. Pour mixture over anchovies and bake in moderate oven until eggs set, about 30 minutes.

Steamed Filet of Perch, Swedish Style

8 Filets of Perch
    (medium size)
    or 4 large
1 tbsp. chopped Parsley
1 tsp. chopped Dill
½ cup Butter
½ cup Fish bouillon
    (or water)
Paprika — Pepper — Salt

Cut fish away from skin and place filets in buttered baking dish, thick edge up. Sprinkle with salt, pepper, paprika, dill and parsley. Melt butter in fish bouillon and pour over. Cover and steam about ten minutes. Serve hot from baking dish.

Baked Mackerel

2 lbs. Mackerel
1 cup Cream
Paprika
1 Lemon

Split and bone fish. Season well. Bake in hot oven 15 minutes. Pour cream over fish and bake 10 minutes longer, basting frequently. Garnish with paprika and sliced lemon.

Boiled Salmon

2 lbs. Fresh Salmon
1 Lemon (sliced)
1 small Carrot
1 spray Fresh Dill
1 spray Tarragon
Few Celery Tops
Salt — Pepper

Scrape clean and wipe salmon. Steam slowly in small amount of water to which have been added the various ingredients, from 35 to 45 minutes. Place on napkin covering platter. Serve with Hollandaise sauce.

Salmon Pudding No. 1

1½ lbs. Salmon
1 cup Rice
1 qt. Milk
2 Eggs
Salt — Pepper

Parboil rice in salted water. Strain and rinse off all starch in additional hot water. Cut salmon in ¼ inch slices. In a well buttered baking dish alternate layers of rice and salmon. Season with salt and pepper. Mix eggs with milk and pour over fish. Bake in moderate oven 45 minutes. Serve in baking dish with melted butter.

Salmon Pudding No. 2

1 lb. Salmon
2 cups Sliced Raw Potatoes
2 cups Milk
2 Eggs
Paprika
Salt — Pepper

Proceed as in Salmon Pudding No. 1, using sliced raw potatoes instead of rice. Any fish may be used in the same manner. If desired, fish broth and part cream may be used in custard.

Smoked Salmon with Eggs and Spinach
(Rökt Lax med Spenat och Ägg)

2 lbs. Salmon (Nova Scotia preferred)
3 lbs. Spinach
6 Eggs
1 small loaf White Bread
Parsley or Dill

Cut crust from bread. Spread with soft butter and sprinkle with finely chopped parsley or dill. Roll sliced smoked salmon in nice shapes and place on bread sockel. Fill spinach (Swedish style) in buttered individual molds and turn out on platter around the sockel. Poach eggs in milk and place between spinach molds. Garnish with dill or parsley and serve.

Pickled Salmon

2 lbs. Fresh Salmon
1 Lemon (sliced)
1 small Carrot
1 spray Fresh Dill
Few Celery Tops
3 tbsp. Tarragon Vinegar
2 Bay Leaves
1 tsp. Gelatin
Salt — Pepper

Clean and split, bones and cut salmon in 2-inch squares. Boil slowly in small amount of water with ingredients about 25 minutes. Place fish in mold. Boil fish broth down until there is just enough to fill mold. Add soaked gelatin. Strain over fish and cool. Place in icebox until firm.

Whole Salmon with Mayonnaise

1 Whole Salmon (5 to 6 lbs.)
3 sprays Dill
1 Lemon, sliced
10 Whole Allspice
2 Bay Leaves
2 cups Mayonnaise
1 tbsp. Gelatin
Truffles, Tarragon Leaves, Stuffed Olives, Hard-boiled Eggs, etc.

Split and bone salmon leaving head whole. Boil bones and fins in water with bay leaves, allspice, lemon, salt, pepper, and some fresh or dry dill. Place the 2 fish halves on fish-rack—one half with skin side down, and the other half with skin side up. Pour broth over carefully. Boil slowly 30 to 45 minutes or until soft, according to size. Boil head and tail 15 minutes with bones and take out carefully. Let fish cool in broth. When cold, lift up strainer and drain. Place halves together like a whole fish. Take skin off fish. Put head and tail in place. Add to Mayonnaise enough melted gelatin to make dressing keep its shape, and pimento to make it salmon-colored. Cover fish with mayonnaise, leaving head and tail plain. Decorate nicely with truffles, Tarragon leaves, sliced stuffed olives, hardboiled eggs, or anything preferred.

Marinated Salmon (Gravlax)

5 lbs. Salmon
1 cup Olive Oil
½ cup Salt
½ cup Sugar
1 tsp. White Pepper
1 tsp. Allspice
Few sprays Fresh Dill
Pinch of Saltpeter

Select middle piece of a 5-lb. salmon. Split and bone. Mix together salt, sugar, saltpeter, white pepper and crushed allspice. Rub oil on both sides of fish halves and season well, placing sprays of dill on top. Place both halves together in a pan and put in light press from 24 to 36 hours. Slice. Serve with Gravlax-sauce "see Sauces", creamed potatoes or spinach. (Swedish style.)

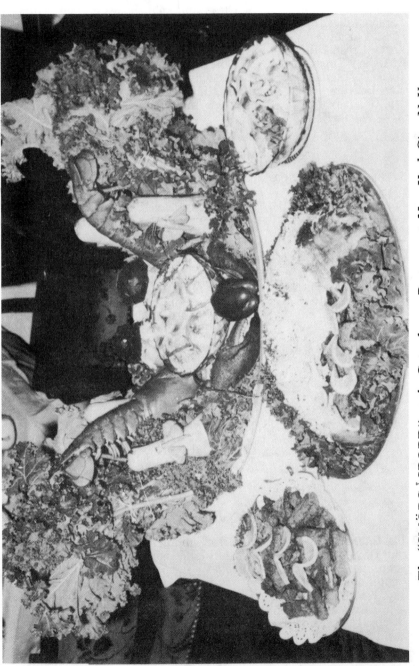

The "SMÖRGÅSBORD" at the Copenhagen Restaurant, New York City, N.Y.

Macaroni and Salmon Pudding

2 lb. Salmon (Cooked, fresh or canned)
4 cups Cooked Macaroni, cut
2 Eggs
1 tbsp. Chopped Onions
1 tbsp. Chopped Celery
1 tbsp. Chopped Green Pepper
1 tbsp. Parsley
1 tsp. Paprika
½ cup Melted Butter
3 cups Milk
½ cup Chopped Olives or Pickles
Salt to taste
1 Lemon

Plunge macaroni in boiling water, but do not cook too long. Strain, cool and cut in ¼ inch rings. Add salmon which has been picked and boned, mix egg-yolks with milk and add all other ingredients. Fold stiffly beaten whites last. Butter a baking dish and fill with mixture. Bake in moderate oven 30 to 40 minutes. Serve with melted butter seasoned with lemon juice.

Codfish au Gratin

3 cups Codfish (Pick from head and bones of left-over fish)
2 cups Cream Sauce
Parmesan Cheese

Place fish in buttered baking dish. Cover with sauce. Sprinkle with Parmesan cheese and brown in moderate oven for 20 minutes. (Haddock can be used in the same manner.)

Baked Cod, Bass or Haddock with Oysters

3 lbs. Fish
1 pt. Oysters
2 Bay Leaves
6 Whole Allspice
Dash of Tabasco
Salt — Pepper

Split, skin and bone fish, leaving two whole filets. Place in buttered baking dish. Boil oysters in juice one minute; remove oysters. Boil fish bones and head in oyster juice with seasoning, 30 minutes. Strain over fish and bake about 20 minutes. Then arrange oysters on top, dust with buttered crumbs, and bake 5 minutes longer.

Creamed Finnan Haddie

2 lbs. Finnan Haddie
¼ lb. Butter
1 tsp. Grated Onions
2 tbsp. Flour
1 tbsp. Lemon Juice
1 tsp. Sugar
Dash of Tabasco
Salt — Pepper

Boil fish in water 15 minutes. Strain and cool. Pick fish from skin and bones. Melt butter. Add flour and enough rich milk to make a thick sauce. Add other ingredients and boil 5 minutes. Fold in the picked fish. Heat and serve. One or two egg-yolks improve the flavor and richness, if desired. Heat, but do not boil.

Plain Boiled Shrimps

2 lbs. Shrimps
4 tbsp. Salt
Few sprays Fresh Dill

Wash shrimps well. Cover with boiling water, add salt and dill and boil from 12 to 15 minutes depending upon size. Let cool in same water. Peel and remove black sand vein. Chill and serve plain or marinate in French dressing.

Shrimps a la Newburg

2 cups boiled and cleaned
    Shrimps (medium or
    small)
3 tbsp. Butter
1½ cups Cream or Rich Milk
3 Egg Yolks
1 wine glass Sherry
Few grains Cayenne
Salt and Pepper

Heat shrimps in butter. Pour cream over, add seasoning and simmer slowly. Add sherry gradually, then egg yolks mixed with part of cream. Season and serve hot with toast. Do not allow mixture to boil after egg yolks are added.

Mock Turtle Stew

2 cans Mock Turtle Soup
1 small can Norwegian
    Fish Balls
12 tiny Potatoes (boiled)
Fricadellen
1 lb. ground Veal
1 cup soft Crumbs
1 Egg
1 tbsp. Chopped Parsley
1 cup Milk
1 tsp. Paprika
Salt and Pepper to taste.

Prepare Fricadellen by mixing the ground veal with the other ingredients. Store in a cool place for an hour or more. Make tiny balls of the mixture and cook in soup a few minutes. Cut fish balls in four pieces and add with the potatoes to the soup.

44

Beef Dishes

Hints and Suggestions

For Swedish Beefsteak, the best results may be obtained by frying in olive oil or a very good salad oil. Oil may be heated to a much higher degree than fat or butter without burning and the meat will retain its rich substance.

Never jab a fork into meat. Turn only once when frying or broiling.

When soup stock is not available use water and Bouillion cubes.

Swedish Meatballs "Köttbullar No. I	Beef Kidney No. I
Swedish Meatballs "Köttbullar No. 2	Beef Kidney No. 2
Meat Loaf "Köttfärs"	Swedish Beefsteak
Whole Beef Roulade	Chateau-Briand Scandia
Beef a la Lindström	Goulash
Individual Beef Roulade	Beef Stew "Kalops"
Stuffed Cabbage "Kåldolma"	Beef Saute Straganoff
Stuffed Cabbage with Rice	Potted Beefsteak
Stuffed Cabbage with Veal and Rice	
Meat Pudding	Beefsteak with Onion Sauce
Beef, Ham and Mushroom Pie	Steak Saute Lyonnaise
Plain Ox Tongues	Seamen's Beef "Sjömans Biff"
Swedish Pot Roast "Grytstek"	Liver Loaf
Ox Tongue with String Beans	Liver Pudding "Korvkaka"

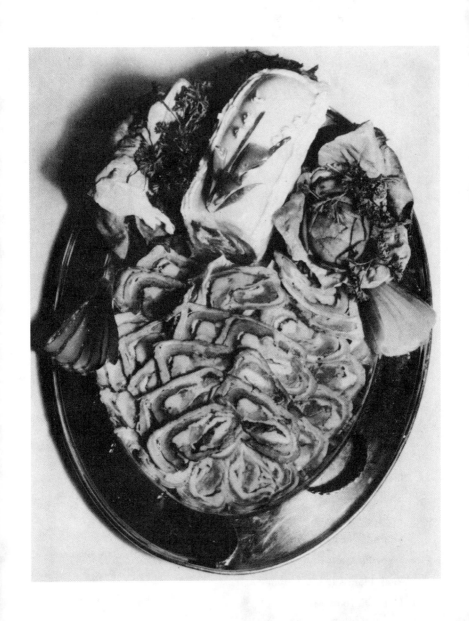

Veal Roulade

Swedish Meatballs (Köttbullar) No. 1

1 lb. Roundsteak
½ lb. Lean Pork
½ cup Chopped Onions
½ cup Bread Crumbs, or 1
    cup of Raw Grated
    Potatoes
2 cups Milk or Water
2 Egg-yolks, 1 White
Salt and Pepper to taste

Grind beef and pork two or three times together. Saute onions and mix with meat and other ingredients. Work mixture 15 minutes. Put in icebox for at least 2 hours. Roll into balls—fry in hot fat or butter, browning balls all around. Deep fat frying makes them brown outside, and tasty and moist inside. Serve with or without brown gravy made of stock.

Swedish Meatballs (Köttbullar) No. 2

1 lb. Round Steak
1 lb. Veal
1 lb. Fresh Pork
½ Loaf White Bread
1 pt. Milk
1 pt. Beer
1 cup grated Onions
1 cup grated raw Potatoes
1 tbsp. Sugar
1 tbsp. Salt or more
½ tsp. Pepper
Oil, Fat, or Butter,
    or mixed

Cut crust from bread and soak in milk one hour. Grind meat 2 or 3 times with onions and potatoes. Mix with other ingredients. Add more seasoning if necessary. Make medium sized balls and fry in deep fat or frying pan. Make gravy from stock and part evaporated milk, or serve meatballs plain with brown beans.

Meat-Loaf (Köttfärs)

Same ingredients as for
    Swedish Meatballs

Prepare exactly the same as meatballs. Shape into loaf and roast in oven about 1 hour.

Whole Beef Roulade

3 lbs. Beef (Topround)
1 lb. Chopped Veal
1 cup Chopped Onions
½ cup White Bread
    Crumbs
1 Egg
1 cup Ketchup
Pinch Cayenne
Salt and Pepper to taste

Pound 1½ inch slice of beef to half an inch thickness. Mix ground veal with ingredients and spread over beef. Roll and tie with string which has been dipped in boiling water. Rub outside with flour mixed with salt and pepper. Brown in hot oven Reduce heat, and roast 1½ hours in moderate oven. Slice, and serve hot with brown gravy; or, serve cold with piquant sauce.

Beef a la Lindström

2 lbs. good Beef
3 Egg Yolks
1 cup Cream or Milk
2 tbsp. Onions
1 cup Boiled Potatoes
1 cup Boiled Beets
1 tbsp. Capers
Salt and Pepper
Butter

Grind meat 3 or 4 times. Cut potatoes and beets into very small cubes. Chop onions and capers. Mix all ingredients together. Season well with salt and pepper. Shape oblong cakes 1¼ inches thick and fry in hot fat one minute on each side. Serve hot.

Individual Beef Roulade

3 lbs. Beef (Topround)
1 cup Chopped Onions
½ cup Chopped Parsley
Flour, Salt, Pepper
Larding Pork

Pound topround to half inch thickness, and 3 inches in diameter. Roll strips of larding pork into mixed chopped onions, parsley, salt and pepper. Place on meat and roll together; tie with string, roll in flour, brown in Dutch Oven on all sides, baste with hot stock or water, and let simmer about 1 hour. Serve with brown gravy made in frying pot.

Stuffed Cabbage (Kåldolma) No. 1

1 head Cabbage
1½ lb. Beef
½ cup Grated Onions
2 cups Stock
Salt — Pepper

After removing stalk, boil whole cabbage 10 to 20 minutes or long enough to separate leaves. Cool. Grind beef, add stock, onions, and seasoning. Fill each cabbage leaf with one tbsp. of mixture, folding leaf neatly around meat. Place in buttered roasting pan. Brown on both sides in hot oven. Reduce heat and cook about 1 hour. Baste with stock or hot water.

Stuffed Cabbage (Kåldolma) No. 2

1 large head of Cabbage
1 lb. ground Beef
½ lb. ground Veal
2 tbsp. Rice
2 cups rich Milk
½ cup grated onions
½ tsp. Celery Salt
1 tbsp. Sugar
Pepper and Salt to Taste

If Cabbage is very young boil only 5 to 8 minutes. If late in season it takes 15 to 20 minutes to get leaves separated, cut heavy stock out with pointed knife. Boil rice in two quarts of water 15 minutes, strain and let hot water run thru strainer to get starch out of rice. Work meat well together with seasoning then add rice and salt and pepper to flavor it right Proceed as in No. 1.

Stuffed Cabbage with Rice (Kåldolma med ris)

1 lb. Ground Veal
1 cup Parboiled Rice
2 cups Milk
1 tbsp. Chutney Sauce
Salt — Pepper

Mix all ingredients. Salt and pepper to taste. Proceed same as for Stuffed Cabbage in preceding recipe.

Meat Pudding

3 cups left-over Meat
   (Ground)
3 cups Mixed Vegetables
   cut fine (Boiled)
2 cups Gravy
½ cup Buttered Bread
   Crumbs
Salt — Pepper

Alternate layers of meat and vegetables in buttered baking dish. Season each layer. Then pour over gravy, cover with buttered bread crumbs, and bake in moderate oven from 20 to 30 minutes.

Beef, Ham and Mushroom Pie

1½ lb. Beef Filet
1 lb. Corned or Smoked
   Ham
18 large Mushrooms
½ cup Bouillon
2 tbsp. Butter
½ cup Sherry
1 tbsp. Flour
Dash of Pepper
Salt if necessary

Cut filet in slices, 2 inches square and ½ inch thick. Cut ham same size only ¼ inch thick. Select mushrooms about same size. Cut off stems and chop, but leave caps whole. Fry ham first, then beef in very hot pan one minute on each side. Keep ham and beef warm. Fry mushroom caps 1½ min. on each side and keep with meat. Slightly brown the chopped stems, add flour, bouillon and sherry and let simmer. In a deep pie dish place ham, beef and mushrooms alternately, overlapping like a border until dish is full. Pour sauce over and cover with a light flaky crust. Brush top with egg yolk and bake in a hot oven until crust is light brown.

Plain Ox Tongues

1 Ox Tongue (Pickled or
   Smoked)
Cabbage Leaves
Parsley or Green Pepper
Bay Leaves
Allspice
Salt — Pepper

Boil a smoked or pickled ox tongue with a few bay leaves and allspice until tender. Skin and trim. Cool in the broth. When ready to use, wipe with towel and slice. Arrange on large platter to resemble the whole tongue. Garnish with large cabbage leaves sprinkled with parsley or green pepper.

Swedish Pot Roast (Grytstek)

4 lbs. Top Round
1 cup Carrots
1 cup Parsnips
1 cup Potatoes
1 cup Small White Onions, peeled
3 Bay Leaves
½ cup Chili Sauce
10 Whole Allspice
3 Whole Anchovies
Season to taste

Select loaf-shaped piece of top round. Have butcher lard and tie. Rub with mixed salt, pepper, paprika and flour. Brown in beef fat on all sides. Reduce heat. Baste with hot stock or water. Let simmer under cover, allowing 20 to 25 minutes to each pound. With a French vegetable cutter, scoop out the different vegetables. Thirty minutes before the meat is done, add the vegetables. Place meat on platter, arranging vegetables neatly in separate heaps. Thicken sauce with small amount of flour. Add chili sauce and water to make medium thick gravy. Strain, and serve separate. If preferred, add a little cream or condensed milk.

Ox Tongue with String Beans

1 Ox Tongue (Pickled)
1 lb. String Beans
3 cups Clear Stock
1 tbsp. Gelatin
1 tbsp. Sugar
1 tbsp. Lemon Juice
2 tbsp. White Vinegar
1 tbsp. Chopped Gherkins
1 tbsp. Capers
Salt — Pepper

Boil slowly a pickled ox-tongue until tender. Skin and trim. Cut tongue in thin oblong slices. Place boiled and marinated string beans crosswise and roll in tongue so that ½ inch extends on both sides. Arrange nicely on serving platter. To 3 cups of clear stock add melted gelatin, sugar, lemon juice, vinegar, gherkins and capers. Salt and pepper to taste. When cooled, pour around meat on platter. Place in refrigerator until ready to serve.

Beef Kidney No. 1

2 large Beef Kidneys
2 cups Milk
½ cup Onions
½ cup Green Pepper
1 tsp. Celery Salt
1 tsp. Paprika
1 tsp. Worcestershire Sauce
1 tbsp. Flour
1 tsp. Salt
1 cup Tomato Juice
Stock
Butter or Fat
Salt

Select young beef kidneys and cut in thin slices. Omit hard fat sinews. Soak in milk one hour or more. In a saucepan cook all ingredients together (except flour) 15 minutes. Drain kidneys, dry in towel, and roll in flour mixed with salt. Brown in butter or fat about 12 to 15 minutes using an iron frying pan. Pour other ingredients over, cook one minute. Season more if necessary and serve hot.

Beef Kidney No. 2

2 young Beef Kidneys
2 cups Milk
½ lb. Lean Bacon
½ lb. Mushrooms
1 cup Soup Stock
½ cup Cream or
    Evaporated Milk
1 tbsp. Chutney

Cut the kidneys in thin slices. Do not use the fat, hard part. Soak in milk 1 or 2 hours. Drain and dry on a towel. Cut bacon in tiny strips crossways. Fry bacon and kidney in an iron frying pan 10 minutes. Add sliced mushrooms. Cook 5 minutes, then add rest of ingredients. Season more if necessary and serve hot.

Swedish Beefsteak

3 lbs. Shortloin (first rib-
    cut)
1½ cups Sliced Onions
Oil, Fat, or Butter
Salt — Pepper

Cut meat from rib and slice in ¾ inch pieces. Pound with cleaver to ½ inch thickness. Brown on both sides in very hot oil, fat, or butter. Sprinkle with salt and pepper. Season onions with salt, pepper, pinch of sugar, and paprika and fry in sep-arate pan. After steak has been removed, cook onions for 1 minute in beefsteak pan with ½ cup bouillon or good stock. Pour over steak and serve immediately.

Chateau-Briand Scandia

2 lbs. Beef Tenderloin
1 can Artichoke Bottoms
1 Truffle
1 glass Sherry
Salt — Pepper

Cut tenderloin of beef into pieces 1 inch thick and 2 inches in diameter. Heat artichoke bottoms in own juice. Strain and keep hot. Fry filets in very hot fat and add seasoning. Place filets on the artichokes and pour truf-fle sauce over or around filets. Truffle sauce is made of very strong bouillon thickened with very little cornstarch. Season with salt, pepper, sherry, and finely chopped truffles.

Goulash

3 lbs. Beef
1 cup Diced Onions
1 cup Diced raw Potatoes
½ cup Chili Sauce
1 tsp. Paprika
2 Bay Leaves
Salt and Pepper
Fat and Stock

Select good tender meat without bones. Cut in strips 1 inch by ½ inch. Brown in fat until light brown, add onions, potatoes and bay leaves, paprika and chili sauce. Pour on suffi-cient stock or water to cover the meat. Simmer slowly under cover for one to two hours or until meat is tender. Serve hot in its own gravy.

Beef Stew (Kalops)

3 lbs. Top Round or Plate
1½ tbsp. Flour
½ tsp. Salt
1 cup Chopped Onions
2 Bay Leaves
6 Allspice
6 White Peppers
½ cup Tomato Pulp
Salt and Pepper
Fat

Slice meat and pound into ½ inch thicknesses. Cut into 2 inch squares. Mix flour and salt and dip meat in it. Fry in fat or butter and place meat in an iron pot. Add onions, tomato pulp and enough water to barely cover. Tie bay leaf, allspice and white pepper in a cloth and put in pot. Cover pot and simmer slowly 1 to 2 hours until meat is well done. Remove bag of spices. If sauce is not of right consistency, add flour or water as desired. Serve hot. If too much fat, skim.

Beef Saute Straganoff

1½ lb. Tenderloin of Beef, diced or cubed (Use trimmings)
2 tbsp. Onions, Chopped
1 cup or small can Tomato Puree
1 tsp. Worcestershire Sauce or Soy (Fuji)
2 tbsp. Butter
1 tbsp. Flour
Pinch Celery Salt
Cayenne
1 glass Madeira or Sherry
Salt and Pepper to taste

Saute cubed or sliced tenderloin on hot fire to brown (not over 3 to 4 minutes). Sprinkle flour and stir well. Then add all other ingredients, and let simmer for 10 to 15 minutes. Add wine and serve very hot.

Potted Beef Steak

3 lbs. seasoned Round or Sirloin Steak, 1½ to 2 inches thick
1 Onion
1 Carrot
2 Bay Leaves
6 Allspice
Salt and Pepper

Broil or fry slices of meat in hot fat on both sides. Sprinkle with salt and pepper and place in a deep iron pot. Add 2 cups stock or water, with onions, carrot and spices. Cook slowly on top of stove or in moderate hot oven about one hour or until meat is tender. Serve with baked macaroni.

Beefsteak with Onion Sauce

3 lbs. Sirloin
or any tender cut
2 cups Onions, Sliced
1 tbsp. Flour
2 cups Rich Milk
Salt, Pepper, and Paprika

Cut meat into even pieces and pound to ½ inch thickness. Fry on both sides in hot butter and place on platter. Fry onions to a golden brown. Add flour, milk, paprika, salt and pepper to taste; cook 5 minutes and pour around meat.

Steak Saute Lyonnaise

1 cup Beef Sauce
2 cups left-over Beef
½ cup sliced Onions
2 cups Potatoes
1 tbsp. Chives
1 tsp. Sat, pinch Pepper
1 tbsp. Chili Sauce

Cut left-over Beef and potatoes in 1 inch strips. Saute onions; add beef sauce, chili sauce, salt and pepper, then potatoes. Heat. Add beef. If roast beef is used, do not boil "just heat" as boiling it will make rare meat tough.

Seamen's Beef (Sjömans Biff)

3 lbs. Top Round
2 lbs. Potatoes (Raw)
2 cups Sliced Onions
3 cups Stock
Salt — Pepper

Prepare same as Swedish Beefsteak. Brown in very hot fat or butter. In baking dish alternate layers of peeled sliced potatoes, meat, and onions. Season each layer. Top layer should be potatoes. Cover with stock. Cook in moderate oven for 1 hour with cover on. Serve from baking dish, if convenient.

Liver Loaf

½ lb. Liver
½ lb. fat, fresh Pork
1 large Onion
1 Egg
2 slices stale White Bread
Milk
Nutmeg — Pepper — Salt

Soak bread in milk. Put liver, pork and onion through meat chopper. Mix with soaked bread, and season. Line a baking dish with bacon, pour in mixture and bake until firm—about half an hour.

Liver Pudding (Korvkaka)

1 cup Rice
3 pts. Milk
3 cups Boiled Calf or
    Beef Liver
1 cup Ham, Pork or Beef
    Fat (left-overs)
1 medium sized Onion
1 tsp. Ground Ginger
½ tsp. Mace
2/3 cup Molasses or 1 cup
    Corn Syrup
1 cup Seedless Raisins
Pepper — Salt — Butter

Boil rice with milk in double boiler until a little more than half done. Cool. Grind liver, onions and fat and mix with rice and all other ingredients. Add pepper and salt and taste carefully, adding more seasoning if necessary. Butter casserole dish, fill with mixture and bake about one hour until pudding is firm and brown. Serve hot with melted butter and Swedish Lingon. Slice left-over liver pudding. Fry and serve with Lingon.

Head Cheese

Veal Dishes

Veal Birds No. 1 "Kalf-Kyckling"	Veal Kidney Saute
Veal Birds No. 2 "Kalf-Kyckling"	Veal Kidney Balls
Veal Birds No. 3 "Kalf-Kyckling"	Veal Balls
Veal Filet De Luxe	Veal Kidneys and Tenderloin
Stuffed Breast of Veal	Veal and Kidney with Mushrooms
Veal in Aspic	Veal Kidneys with Rice
Veal Cutlets	Creamed Sweetbreads
Veal Roulade	Sweetbreads with Mushrooms
Veal Fricadellen	Sweetbreads with Celery Root

Veal Birds No. 1 (Kalv-Kyckling)

2½ lbs. Leg of Veal
½ cup White Bread
    Crumbs (fresh)
1 cup Milk
1 Egg-yolk
1 tsp. Escoffier Sauce
½ tsp. Paprika
Few Grains Cayenne
½ cup Butter
t tbsp. Flour
1 cup Cream
Salt — Pepper

Have the butcher slice veal ½ inch thick, and flatten it down to ¼ inch with cleaver; cut into pieces 3 x 4 inches, and grind trimmings through meat grinder 2 or 3 times. (This will save work and time.) Mix well ground meat with crumbs, milk, egg and seasoning, and spread a thin layer on meat. Roll and tie each one with string. Brown birds in butter in Dutch oven; baste with stock or milk and simmer slowly 1 hour. Remove strings. Add flour and cream in pan. Replace birds, heat and serve in gravy.

Veal Birds No. 2 (Kalv-Kyckling)

2 lbs. Leg of Veal
2 tbsp. Parmesan Cheese
1 tsp. Sugar
2 tsp. Salt
¼ tsp. Pepper
Few grains Cayenne
1 cup Butter
1 cup Chopped Parsley
1 tbsp. Flour
1 cup Cream
Broth or Milk

Proceed as in recipe No. 1 omitting ground meat for stuffing. Mix cheese, sugar, salt, pepper, and cayenne together and sprinkle on meat. Mix parsley in half of the cold butter; place a tsp. of this on each slice of veal and roll tight. Tie with string and brown in remaining butter. Baste with broth or hot milk and cook slowly 1 hour, or until meat is tender. Take out birds and remove strings— keep hot. Make gravy in pan, adding flour and cream. Season to taste, strain, and serve separate, or pour sauce over meat.

Veal Birds No. 3 (Kalv-Kyckling)

8 or 10 Thin slices of
    Veal (4 x 5)
1 cup raw ground Ham
1 cup All Bran
½ cup Chopped Celery
1 tbsp. Chopped Green
    Pepper
1 tbsp. Chopped Olives
Salt and Pepper

Mix bran, celery, green pepper and olives with ground ham and let stand one hour to swell. Shake a little salt, pepper and paprika on veal slices. Spread mixture on veal and roll and tie with strings or fasten with toothpicks. Brown in a hot oven, reduce heat and cook from 1 to 1½ hours. Remove strings or toothpicks. If desired, make gravy in roasting pan using 1 tablespoon flour; add stock, milk and cream. Season with salt, pepper and paprika and strain over meat.

Veal Filet De Luxe

1 Veal Filet (1½ to 2 lbs.)
1 can Artichoke Bottoms
3 tbsp. Butter
1 tbsp. Flour
½ cup Cream
1 Truffle
1 wineglass Madeira or
    Sherry
Salt — Pepper

Cut filets in 1-inch pieces; flatten a little and fry. Heat artichokes in liquid. Place artichokes on platter with one filet on each. Make gravy with flour, cream and liquid from artichoke bottoms. Season well with salt and pepper. Add thinly sliced or chopped truffles, and cook 5 minutes. Add sherry or Madeira and cook 1 minute longer. Pour around meat on platter.

Stuffed Breast of Veal

1 Breast of Milk Veal
    4 to 5 lbs.
2 Veal Kidneys
1 cup Soft White
    Bread crumbs
1 cup milk
2 Eggs
1 cup Ham or Tongue
½ cup chopped Onions
1 tbsp. chopped Pimento
1 tbsp. salt (or more)
1 tbsp. Sugar
½ tsp. Pepper
½ tsp. Paprika

Select a good, white breast of Veal. Carefully cut out rib bones leaving the meat whole. Grind kidneys, mix well with all ingredients (except ham) to a smooth fine dough. Spread on breast; sprinkle ham or tongue (previously cut in narrow strips). Roll meat together. Tie carefully with string and roast in moderate oven from one to two hours depending on meat. Serve with Lingon and Cucumbers Swedish Style.

Veal in Aspic

3 lbs. Veal (Forequarters)
4 Bay Leaves
10 Allspice
4 Cloves
Pickled Beets
Seasoning

Wash meat and cover with cold water, to which has been added 1 tsp. salt. Let come to boil and skim well. Add bay leaves, allspice, and cloves. Let simmer about 1½ hours, or until soft. Strain stock into another pan. Pick meat from bones when cool, and cut in cubes, chop, or grind—as desired. Boil bones with liquid until there is just enough stock to cover meat. Strain over meat and let come to a boil. Season to taste. Pour into molds. When cold, let stand in refrigerator until firm. Serve with vinegar and pickled beets.

Veal Cutlets

2 lbs. Sliced Leg of Veal
½ cup Grated Parmesan
    Cheese
2 cups Sliced Carrots
1 cup Orange Juice
4 tbsp. Sherry
1 tbsp. Salt
1 tsp. Paprika
¼ tsp. Pepper
1 tsp. Sugar
1 cup Stock

Mix cheese, salt, pepper, paprika, and sugar. Dip meat in this mixture and brown in butter on both sides. Let simmer slowly for 30 minutes. Cover meat with carrots sliced crosswise ¼ inch thick. Pour orange juice and stock over meat. Simmer under cover 30 minutes, or until carrots are cooked. Pour sherry over carrots and cook a few more minutes.

Veal Roulade

4 lbs. Flank Milk Veal
½ cup Butter
½ cup Pistachio Nuts
    blanched and crushed
2 tbsp. Chopped Green
    Peppers
2 tbsp. Chutney
1 tbsp. Salt
1 tsp. Curry Powder
1 tsp. Paprika

Split meat, making two rolls, so as to make neat slices. Mix all spices and spread over meat. Roll and tie well with string. Simmer slowly in water or stock (just enough to cover meat) for about 1 hour. Place in press over night.

Veal Fricadellen

1 lb. Veal (well ground)
½ Cup Crumbs
Chicken or Veal Broth
½ cup Cream
1 Egg
½ lb. Mushrooms
½ cup Chopped Parsley
¼ tsp. Mace
Salt — Pepper

Mix veal with crumbs, broth, egg-yolk, mace, salt and pepper. Fold in stiffly beaten eggwhites. Make small, round balls and cook slowly in stock, enough to cover, for 30 minutes. Thicken sauce with 1 tbsp. flour. Add sauted mushrooms, parsley, cream and season to taste.

Veal Kidney Saute

2 Veal Kidneys
1 wineglass Sherry
2 tbsp. Butter
½ cup Flour
1 tsp. Salt
½ tsp. Sugar
¼ tsp. Pepper
¼ tsp. Paprika

Leave thin layer of fat around veal kidney. Slice ¼ inch thick. Dip in flour mixed with dry ingredients and fry in butter. Place on serving platter. Pour off fat from skillet with exception of 1 tbsp. Add sherry Bring to boil and pour over kidneys.

Veal Kidney Balls

2 Veal Kidneys (with fat)
2 Eggs
1 cup White Bread Crumbs
Celery Salt
⅓ tsp. Paprika
Salt
Pepper to taste

Have kidneys ground twice including small layer of surrounding fat. Mix with egg, crumbs, and seasoning. Let stand 1 hour in refrigerator. Make small balls and fry in remaining kidney fat or butter. Serve hot.

Veal Balls

1 lb. Veal
½ cup White Br. Crumbs
2 Eggs
1 cup Grated Raw Carrots
½ cup chopped Olives or
  Mixed Pickles
½ tsp. Paprika
Butter or Fat
2 cups Tomato Soup
Salt and Pepper

Ground veal very fine and mix with crumbs, egg, carrots, paprika, salt, and pepper to taste. Add enough stock or water to make a soft dough. Let stand in icebox one hour or more. Fry small balls in butter or fat, when ready pour tomato soup over. Simmer slowly for 15 minutes.

Veal Kidneys and Tenderloin

2 Veal Kidney
1 Veal or Pork Tenderloin
4 Raw Potatoes (Medium
  size)
2 tbsp. Finely Chopped
  Scallions
1 cup Chicken or Veal
  Stock
3 tbsp. Sherry
Salt — Pepper —

Place in buttered baking dish a layer of sliced potatoes, a layer of tenderloin and kidneys both sliced thin. Sprinkle with chopped scallions. Repeat until all are used. Season each layer. Top layers should be potatoes. Pour over a cup of stock and bake in moderate oven for 1 hour. Take out dish and add wine. Bake 10 minutes longer. Serve in dish.
Or, fry sliced kidney and tenderloin first, use boiled potatoes and proceed as above, bake half hour.

Veal and Kidney with Mushrooms

1½ lbs. Veal Tenderloin
2 Veal Kidneys
½ lb. Mushrooms
½ cup Madeira
1 cup Cream
1 tbsp. Flour
1 tsp. Paprika
Salt and Pepper

Cut tenderloin in half-inch pieces and slice kidneys crossways quarter inch thick, leaving a narrow strip of fat around. Leave mushrooms whole or slice if large. Dip veal and kidney slices in flour and fry slowly about 7 minutes on each side. Place on hot platter, alternating slices. Saute mushrooms in same pan five minutes. Stir in flour, pour cream over, add paprika, salt and pepper to taste. Warm wine and add gradually. Stir while heating. Pour sauce around meat and serve hot.

59

Veal Kidneys with Rice

2 Veal Kidneys
½ cup Rice
1 cup Stock
½ cup Cream
Salt — Pepper — Paprika
⅓ cup Butter

Wash rice and boil 15 minutes. Put in strainer and pour hot water over rice. Season with salt, pepper, pinch of sugar, and ⅓ cup of butter. Fill in well buttered ring mold. Place in pan of water and heat. Slice veal kidneys, dip in flour and season. Saute in butter. Make gravy with stock and cream. Mix kidneys with gravy. Turn out rice ring on platter and fill center with kidney.

Note: Instead of stock and cream use tomato soup with rice if preferred.

Creamed Sweetbreads

2 pairs Sweetbreads
2 cups Cream Sauce
2 tsp. Escoffier Sauce
½ tsp. Sugar
Salt — Pepper
Pepper and Salt

Parboil sweetbreads 15 or 20 minutes. Plunge in cold water. Carefully pluck the meat from skin and leave pieces as they are. Make rich cream sauce, and add seasoning. Mix sweetbreads in sauce and serve on toast or in pastry shells.

Sweetbreads with Mushrooms

1 pair Sweetbreads
½ lb. Button Mushrooms
1 tbsp. Chutney Sauce
1 wineglass White Wine or
  Sherry
1 cup Cream Sauce
Salt — Pepper

Prepare sweetbreads as in Creamed Sweetbreads. Select white button mushrooms; break off stems, and simmer caps in butter for 10 minutes. Make cream sauce in same pan. Add sweetbreads. Season. Just before serving, add 1 wineglass of white wine or sherry. Serve in pastry shells or on toast.

Sweetbreads with Celery Root

2 pairs Sweetbreads
3 Celery Roots
5 strips Bacon
½ cup Butter
6 or 8 Whole Wheat
  Crackers
Salt — Pepper

Parboil sweetbreads and remove outside skin. Boil celery roots until tender—about 45 minutes. Cool. Peel and cut each root into 2 or 3 slices. Place in baking dish. Cover with a slice of sweetbreads dipped in butter and whole wheat cracker crumbs. Place ½ strip bacon on each. Brown in hot oven or under broiler.

Lamb Dishes

Hints and Suggestions

Lamb is one of the most popular and nutritious meats on the market, and when properly prepared, it is easy to digest. Lamb has a very distinctive flavor from other meats and should never be mixed with other meat-stock for soups and gravies.

Roast Leg of Lamb

Roast Breast of Lamb

Stuffed Breast of Lamb No. 1

Stuffed Breast of Lamb No. 2

Lamb with Cabbage "Får i Kål"

Lamb Roulades

Minced Lamb

Corned Lamb "Rimsaltat Lamm"

Ragout of Lamb

Lamb Kidney Saute

Lamb Meatballs

Lamb with Dill Sauce

Mutton Chops with Pate de Foie Gras

Swedish Lamb Stew

Lamb Pudding

Veal in Jello

Roast Leg of Lamb, Swedish Style

Leg of Lamb
2 tbsp. Chopped Parsley
1 tbsp. Italian Tomato
Paste
½ cup Butter
1 tsp. Celery Salt
1 Bay Leaf
5 Allspice
1 Carrot
1 Onion
Salt — Pepper

Punch 2 rows of holes in leg of lamb. Fill with butter mixed with parsley, tomato paste, celery salt, salt and pepper. Pot roast lamb slowly 1½ hours with bay leaf, allspice, onion, and carrot. Add a little boiling water and bake. When ready, sprinkle flour in pot — enough for a medium thick gravy. Boil and strain.

Roast Breast of Lamb

4 lb. Breast of Lamb
1 tbsp. Chopped Mint
(optional)
1 tbsp. Salt
¼ tsp. Pepper
¼ tsp. Mace
1 tbsp. Sugar
2 tbsp. Flour

Have butcher saw bones carefully, leaving meat whole. Rub meat with a mixture of salt, pepper, sugar, chopped mint, flour, and mace. Brown in hot oven. Baste with lamb fat (no water). Reduce heat and cook slowly for 1½ hours or less.

Stuffed Breast of Lamb No. 1

1 Breast and Belly of Lamb
1 lb. Ground Lamb
1 cup Bread crumbs
1 cup Milk
1 Green Pepper chopped
1 Onion chopped
1 Egg
½ tsp. each of Celery
Salt, Pepper and Mace
1 tbsp. Salt

Select a good sized fresh breast and belly of lamb. Have the butcher bone the meat. Mix salt, pepper, celery salt and mace together. Rub half of this on both sides of meat. Add remainder to ground meat, bread crumbs (previously soaked in milk) egg, onion and green pepper. Work well together; spread evenly on meat. Roll and tie well with string. Roast and serve with or without gravy.

Stuffed Breast of Lamb No. 2

1 Breast of Lamb
2 Lamb Kidneys
Lamb Trimmings
½ cup partially cooked
Green Peas
8 or 10 strips (¼ inch)
parboiled Carrots
½ tsp. Celery Salt
½ tsp. Paprika
1 Egg
1 cup Stock or Milk
Salt and Pepper

Select a large breast of lamb; carefully cut out rib bones and spread meat on table. Grind trimmings from meat with kidneys twice and mix with other ingredients. Spread on meat, then place carrot strips lengthwise on top. Sprinkle peas on and roll breast together. Tie with string and roast in a moderately heated oven 1½ hours, basting with stock or water. Serve hot with creamed vegetables, or cold with salad, or plain on Smörgåsbord.

Lamb with Cabbage *(Får i Kål)*

3 lbs. Shoulder of Lamb
3 lbs. New Cabbage
2 Bay Leaves
6 Allspice
1 tbsp. Salt
1 tsp. Sugar
¼ tsp. Pepper
1 Onion
1 Carrot

Cut lamb as for stew. Melt some lamb fat or butter in Dutch oven. Alternate layers of cabbage and meat, seasoning each layer. Leave onion and carrot whole and remove before serving. Cook slowly from 1 to 2 hours or until meat is tender.

Lamb Roulades

8 or 10 thin slices of Leg of Lamb 3 & 4
4 Lamb Kidneys
½ cup Grape Nuts
1 tbsp. chopped Mixed Pickles
⅓ tsp. chopped Mint
1 cup Milk or Stock
Salt — Pepper

Grind kidneys fine. Mix with other ingredients. Let stand while preparing meat. Wth a cleaver or mallet pound the meat slices to ¼ inch thickness. Sprinkle with Pepper and salt. Spread mixture on top. Roll and tie with strings. Roast in moderate oven about one hour. Serve with or without gravy, or with mint sauce.

Minced Lamb

2 cups Minced Left-over Lamb
2 cups Cooked Rice or Macaroni
1½ cups Lamb Gravy
1 tsp. Chutney
½ tsp. Sugar
Corn Flakes
Salt — Pepper

Cut left over lamb up into fine pieces. Add same amount of rice or finely cut cooked macaroni. Mix with other ingredients, heat and serve with heated corn flakes placed around lamb.

Corned Lamb *(Rimsaltat Lamm)*

5 lb. Leg or Shoulder of Lamb
2 cups Salt
⅓ cup Sugar
1 tsp. Thyme
¼ tsp. Saltpeter
3 Bay Leaves
10 Allspice
10 Whole Black Peppers

Mix 1 cup of salt with other ingredients and rub meat thoroughly with mixture. Make brine with 1 cup of salt and 2 quarts boiled water. When cool, pour brine over meat—placing weight on meat to keep it entirely covered. Let stand in brine from 5 to 7 days. When meat is removed from brine, cover with cold water and let come slowly to a boil. Skim. Boil from 1 to 2 hours, depending on meat. Serve with mashed turnips "Rotmos," mashed potatoes, or boiled vegetables — such as carrots, onions, or parsnips.

Ragout of Lamb

2 cups left-over Lamb
1 cup Lamb Gravy
1 Dill Pickle
1 tbsp. Mixed Pickles
1 cup Boiled Potatoes
   (optional)
2 tbsp. Chili Sauce

Cut meat, potatoes, and pickles in narrow strips one inch long. Heat lamb gravy, add chili sauce, meat and pickles. Let come to a boil and serve hot.

Lamb Pudding

2 cups Minced Lamb
1 cup Lamb Gravy
1 tbsp. A-1 Sauce
1 tbsp. Chili Sauce
1 tsp. Sugar
2 cups Mashed Potatoes

Cube leftover roast lamb. Mix with lamb gravy. Season with salt, pepper, chili sauce, and A-1 or Worcestershire sauce—also sugar. Pour into buttered baking dish. Press mashed potatoes through a pastry tube on top of lamb. Bake in moderate oven from 20 to 30 minutes. Vegetables may be mixed in meat, if preferred.

Lamb Meatballs

1½ lb. Lamb
½ cup Rye Crumbs
2 tbsp. Catsup
⅓ tsp. Ground Mace
1 Egg
1 cup of Beer
Salt — Pepper

Mix all ingredients, add enough water to make a firm dough. Let stand 2 or 3 hours. Make small balls and fry in lamb fat, butter or half and half. This may also be shaped into a loaf and baked.

Lamb with Dill Sauce

1 leg Lamb
3 tbsp. Butter
3 tbsp. Flour
½ cup White Vinegar
   or less
3 tbsp. Sugar
3 tbsp. Chopped Fresh Dill
2 Egg-yolks
Salt — Pepper

Cover with just enough water to steam. Let come to a boil and skim well. Simmer until tender, or about 1½ hours. Melt butter. Add flour and broth to a thick sauce. Add vinegar, sugar, and chopped dill. Salt and pepper to taste. Add egg-yolks last, heat, but do not boil. Slice leg of lamb in thin slices. Pour sauce over lamb, or serve separately. Shoulder may be used instead of leg.

Mutton Chops with Pate de Foie Gras

4 Mutton Chops
4 tsp. Pate de Foie Gras
   or Liverpaste
Salt — Pepper

Cut loin of mutton chops thick (1½ to 2 inches). Make an incision in middle of chop and fill with Pate de Foie Gras or Liverpaste. Bake in very hot oven 10 to 15 minutes. Salt and pepper to taste.

Swedish Lamb Stew

4 or 5 lbs. Shoulder of
  Spring Lamb
1 cup Small Whole Onions
1 cup each Sliced Carrots,
  Parsnips, Potatoes,
  Celery, and Leeks
1 cup Peas
2 cups Canned Tomatoes
½ cup Chopped Parsley
3 Bay Leaves
10 Whole Allspice
Salt — Pepper

Cover meat with cold water. Add 1 tbsp. salt. Let come to a boil and skim well. Add bay leaves and allspice. Simmer 30 minutes. Add vegetables, except peas, and boil slowly for 30 to 40 minutes. Place on platter or in deep dish. Sprinkle with parsley and separate cooked peas. Serve preferably in soup plates with plenty of stock, or on regular plates if desired. When served in soup plates, boil meat whole and cut from bones in 1 inch pieces.

Lamb Kidney Saute

6 Lamb Kidneys
1 cup White Wine
Flour
2 Bay Leaves
6 whole All spice
1 tsp. Chutney
Salt and Pepper

Heat wine with bay leaves and allspice in sauce pan. Let stand while preparing meat. Cut kidney away from fat and melt part of fat in frying pan. Slice kidney thin; dip in flour mixed with salt and pepper. Fry five to eight minutes. Strain wine over kidneys; add chutney; boil one minute and serve hot.

Pork Dishes

Virginia Ham

Ham Loaf

Ham Mousse "Skinkfärs"

Stuffed Loin of Pork "Plommon
    Späckad Fläsk Karre"

Roast Stuffed Suckling Pig
    "Stekt Fyld Späd-Gris"

Roast Stuffed Spare-Ribs
    "Stekt Fyld Revbensspjell"

Fried Side Pork with Onion Sauce

Pork Sausages with Riced Potatoes

Swedish Pork Sausages

Ham Roulade

Ham and Potato Balls

Cold Pork Roulade "Rull-Korv"

Fried Side Pork with Potatoes "Stekt
    Rimsaltat Fläsk med Stuvad
    Potatis"

Pork Tenderloin with Mushrooms

Roast Side of Pork Stuffed with Veal
    "Stekt Färserad Sidfläsk"

Boiled Pigs Feet with Pickled Beets

Broiled Pigs Feet with Sharp Sauce

Head Cheese from Side Pork "Pressylta"

The "SMÖRGÅSBORD" at the Copenhagen Restaurant, New York City, N.Y.

Virginia Ham

1 Virginia Ham (Razor back Smithfield) is good
1 cup Bread Crumbs
1 cup Brown Sugar
Juice of 1 Lemon
1 tbsp. Tarragon Vinegar

Soak ham 2 or 3 days, changing water daily. Boil slowly until the crossbone loosens easily from meat. Let cool in stock over night. With a very sharp knife carefully remove skin and trim off the thin layer of seasoned meat around ham. Mix bread crumbs, brown sugar, lemon juice and vinegar. Spread mixture on ham. Brown in medium hot oven, but do not baste, Serve hot or cold.

Ham Loaf

1½ lbs. Ground Lean Smoked Ham
1½ lbs. Ground Lean Fresh Pork
1½ cups Milk
1 cup Bread Crumbs
2 Eggs
2 Green Peppers, Chopped
2 Large Chopped Onions
2 cups Strained Tomato Juice

Mix all ingredients. Half fill buttered oblong mold. Place dish in hot water and bake slowly 2 hours. Serve hot or cold.

Ham Mousse (Skinkfärs)

3 cups Ground Cooked Ham
½ cup Italian Tomato Puree
1 tsp. Mustard
2 Eggs
1 cup Cream
Dash of Cayenne
1 tbsp. Gelatin
1 tsp. Ground Ginger

Grind ham (preferably Virginia Ham) very fine. Press through sieve and add seasoning. Beat egg-yolks until very light. Add meat and mix well. Add melted gelatin. Fold in whipped cream and, lastly, stiffly beaten eggwhites. Fill fancy mold, Let set. Turn out on platter and garnish. Or make one cup of cream sauce, add egg-yolks but do not boil. Add other ingredients and when cool add gelatin. cream and eggwhites.

Stuffed Loin of Pork (Plommon Späckad Fläsk Karré)

5 to 7 lbs. Loin of Pork
1 cup Prunes
1 tbsp. Salt
1 tsp. Sugar
1 tsp. Ginger
¼ tsp. Pepper

Select a young loin of pork. With a pointed knife, make an incision and fill with prunes (soaked and stoned). Tie. Rub meat with mixed salt, pepper, sugar, and ginger. Roast about 1 hour or until tender. Serve hot or cold. (If served hot, make a light brown gravy with broth made from pork bones.)

Roast Stuffed Suckling Pig (Stekt Fylld Spädgris)

1 Suckling Pig (10 or 12 lbs.)
6 Apples
1 lb. Prunes (stoned)
1 tbsp. Sugar
1 tsp. Ground Ginger
2 tbsp. Salt
½ tsp. Pepper

Clean and wipe pig inside and outside with wet towel dipped in vinegar. (Do not wash.) Mix salt, pepper, sugar, and ginger, and rub inside and outside of pig. Peel, core, and quarter apples; mix with prunes and stuff pig. Sew opening. Place pig on grate in open roasting pan and brown in hot oven. Baste frequently with plenty of fat. Do not allow any water or steam to form, or the skin will burst and spoil the meat. When brown, reduce heat and finish roasting. (About 10 or 12 minutes to each pound.) Remove string. Serve with stuffing, hot or cold.

Roast Stuffed Spare-Ribs (Stekta Fyllda Revbensspjäll)

5 lbs. Fresh Spareribs
1 tbsp. Salt
1 tbsp. Sugar
1 tsp. Cellerysalt
1 tsp. Ground Ginger
¼ tsp. White Pepper
4 Apples (Tart)
1 cup Stoned Prunes

Select large, meaty spareribs. Saw bones carefully, leaving meat whole. Mix salt, sugar, paprika, ginger, and pepper; rub meat well with mixture on both sides. Peel, core, and quarter apples. Fill spareribs with apples and prunes; fold, and tie with string. Brown in Dutch oven, turning frequently. Baste with stock or boiling water, and let simmer slowly for about 2 hours. Remove meat, untie, and keep hot. For gravy, add 1 tbsp. flour, 2 cups rich milk, and boil 5 minutes; strain and serve. May be served cold without gravy.

Fried Side Pork with Onion Sauce

1 lb. Lean Salt Pork
1 cup Sliced Onions
1 tbsp. Flour
2 cups Milk
Salt — Pepper — Paprika

Slice pork ¼ inch thick. Fry slowly until crisp. Pour off most of fat after removing pork. Place sliced onions in frying pan and cook slowly. Add flour, milk, and seasoning. Serve with boiled potatoes.

Ham Roulades

8 or 10 slices Smoked Ham
    about 3 x 4
½ lb. Veal
1 Veal Kidney
4 slices White Bread
1 cup Milk
3 tbsp. Chili Sauce
¼ tsp. Paprika
Salt — Pepper

Remove crusts and soak bread in milk. Grind veal and kidney 3 or 4 times. Mix well with rest of ingredients. Spread on slices of ham. Tie with strings or fasten with toothpicks. Roast in oven. Baste with stock or hot water (a little at a time) and cook from 1 to 1½ hours. Serve with creamed vegetable. For Smörgasbord cut ham in slices 2 x 3 inches and proceed same as above.

Ham and Potato Balls

3 cups Mashed Potatoes
½ cup Ground Ham
    (cooked)
1 Egg
1 tsp. Chopped Parsley
Dash Pepper
1 cup Soft Bread Crumbs

Mix potatoes with ham, egg, parsley and pepper. Make small balls. Roll in crumbs and fry in bacon or other fat, or roll balls in beaten egg, crumbs, and deep fry.

Swedish Pork Sausages

2 lbs. Sausages "fresh"
1 lb. small Potatoes
3 Bay eaves
10 Whole Allspice
2 tbsp. chopped Parsley
2 tbsp. Salt
¼ tbsp. Pepper

Prick the sausages with a needle or sharp fork before placing in cold water to come slowly to a boil. Add seasoning and simmer 20 minutes. Add small peeled potatoes and boil another 20 minutes. Never cover pot and have just enough water to cover. Slice sausages and serve hot with plenty of parsley.

Cold Pork Roulade (Rull-Korv)

5 lbs. Lean Side Pork
½ cup Brown Sugar
1 tbsp. Salt
2 tsp. Ground Ginger
2 tbsp. Chopped Green
    Pepper
12 Whole Allspice
6 Cloves
3 tbsp. Tarragon Vinegar
1 tbsp. Dry Mustard

When selecting pork, see that there are two layers of lean pork. Split side of pork in two, leaving a layer of lean meat on each half. Crush allspice and cloves with rolling pin and mix with other ingredients. Moisten mixture with Tarragon vinegar, and spread on slices of pork. Roll tight and tie with string. Boil slowly in salted water about 1 to 1½ hours. Put in press over night. Cover with brine and place in refrigerator. (Brine should be made of 1 cup salt, 2 tbsp. sugar, 1 cup white vinegar, and enough water to cover the pork.) (One piece of pork may be roasted and served hot.)

Pork Sausages with Riced Potatoes

1 lb. Pork Sausages
2 tbsp. Butter
1 cup Milk
6 Medium Potatoes
Salt — Pepper
1 tbsp. Chopped Parsley

Peel, wash, and slice potatoes. Steam very slowly in milk to which has been added butter, salt, and pepper. Press through potato ricer on serving platter. Broil sausages and arrange around potatoes. (Creamed potatoes may be used instead of riced.) Sprinkle with parsley.

Fried Side Pork with Potatoes
(Stekt Rimsaltat Fläsk med Stuvad Potatis)

½ lb. Lean Salt Pork
2 cups Cold Boiled Potatoes
   (cuber fine)
2 cups Milk
Chopped Parsley
Salt — Pepper —

Slice pork ¼ inch thick. Fry slowly until crisp. Remove pork and keep hot. Pour off most of fat and place in frying pan finely cubed cold potatoes. Cover with milk, and add seasoning. Let simmer slowly until most of milk is absorbed. Sprinkle with parsley and serve with pork. If desired rub slices of pork with dry mustard before frying.

Pork Tenderloin with Mushrooms

2 Pork Tenderloins
1 lb. Fresh Mushrooms
Toast buttered
Salt — Pepper

Cut tenderloins into small 1 inch filets and flatten slightly. Season well. Fry in butter about 15 minutes. Saute or broil mushroom tops. Arrange filets on round slices of toast, and top each one with mushrooms.

Roast Side of Pork Stuffed with Veal
(Stekt Färserat Sidfläsk)

5 to 6 bs. Side of Fresh
   Pork with Ribs
1 lb. Veal (Ground)
1 cup Sifted Bread Crumbs
½ cup Flour
1 tbsp. Salt
1 tbsp. Sugar
1 tsp. Dry Mustard
1 tsp. Ground Ginger
1 tsp. Ground Allspice
1 tsp. Paprika
½ tsp. White Pepper
1 cup Boiled Rice
½ cup Chili Sauce or Catsup
2 Eggs

Order side pork with rind on. Have butcher slit a pocket in middle of meat between rind and ribs for filling. Mix all dry seasoning, and rub meat on outside with part of mixture —using the remainder for stuffing, with veal, bread crumbs, rice, chili sauce or catsup, and eggs. Mix well and fill pocket, sewing opening together. Brown in hot oven with skin side up—preferably scored. Reduce heat and allow from 15 to 20 minutes per pound for roasting. (For gravy, follow recipe for roast spareribs.) Serve hot or cold, preferably with Swedish "Lingon berries."

Boiled Pigs Feet with Pickled Beets

6 Pigs Feet (Salt or Fresh)
1 tsp. Allspice
3 Bay Leaves or 1 tbsp.
   Mixed Spices

Boil Pigs feet with spices in water to which has been added a little baking soda and vinegar (this keeps meat white). Boil until very soft. When cold, serve with pickled beets. (Will keep from 1 to 2 weeks if placed in brine. If fresh pigs feet are used, add 2 tbsp. salt when boiling).

Broiled Pigs Feet with Sharp Sauce

3 Pigs Feet (6 Halves)
1 Egg
1 cup Bread Crumbs
Boiled or Pickled Beets
½ tsp. Dry Mustard
Sharp Sauce

Split cold boiled pigs feet. Dip in beaten egg, and then in bread crumbs to which mustard, salt and pepper have been added. Broil until brown. Serve hot with Sharp Sauce, and beets. (Creamed potatoes may also be served.)

Head Cheese (Pressylta)

3 to 5 lbs. Fresh Side Pork
   or Pigshead
3 lbs. Breast or Shoulder of
   Veal
5 or 6 Bay Leaves
12 Allspice
10 Whole White Peppers
2 tbsp. Salt

Soak pigshead over night and boil 2 hours. Cover with water. Come to boil slowly. Skim well. Add other ingredients and let simmer until meat is soft. Strain and save liquid. Wring out a towel in water and place inside of round mold. Remove skin from pork and place half in bottom of dish (on top of towel). Then alternate with slices of pork and veal. Season well each layer. Top with remainder of pork skin. Gather together edges of towel and tie securely. Place in heated liquid and boil for 15 minutes. Let stand in heavy press over night. Will keep in brine from 1 to 2 weeks. Serve with pickled beets. (If desired, various vegetables may be added while boiling, which greatly improves the flavor.)

Chicken in Chaufroix

Chicken Dishes

Judging from restaurant orders chicken is the most relished and popular meat of all kind. When well prepared it is tasty and easy to digest for young and old. The best and easiest way to prepare small chicken from 1½ to 2½ lbs. apiece is broiling. From 2 to 3 lbs.—frying: larger birds should be roasted. Fowls should be boiled and served with a good parsley or mushroom sauce.

Of course all chickens should be fresh killed if possible Frozen, they loose that delicate flavor — connoisseurs well know and appreciate young chicken should never be plunged in water and washed. Remove all intestines thoroughly then singe and wipe in and outside with wet towel.

Squab Chicken - Swedish Style - "Persilje-Kyckling"

Chicken Fricassee

Steamed Chicken

Fried Chicken "Scandia"

Potted Chicken

Chicken Croquettes

Chicken Croquettes with Rice

Chicken Croquettes with Mushrooms

Chicken Souffle

Chicken and Nut Balls

Chicken Livers with Mushrooms

Chicken Stew - Soup

Blanketed Chicken "Kyckling Frityr"

Chicken Fricassee

1 Fowl
1 Lemon
2 Bay Leaves
6 Allspice
6 Whole White Pepper
1 Onion
1 Carrot
2 Stalks Celery
2 tbsp. Butter
2 tbsp. Flour
2 tbsp. Parsley
1 or 2 Egg Yolks
½ cup Cream or
    Exaporated Milk
Salt and Pepper

Clean chicken well. Rub meat inside and out with lemon to make meat white and tasty. Melt fat and strain. Save liver. Cut leg and second joint together from chicken. Leave the rest whole. Put in a deep narrow pot, legs in bottom and breast on top. Cover with water and a teaspoon salt. Let slowly come to a boil. Skim well two or three times. Then add all seasoning and vegetables. Boil slowly 1½ hours or until breast is tender. Remove breast from bone. Put bones back in pot and boil a little longer until legs are well done. Melt butter or chicken fat; add flour and chicken broth, making a thick gravy. Add chopped parsley and just before serving, add egg yolks mixed with cream. Cut chicken in nice pieces, pour gravy over and serve hot.
If preferred serve gravy from gravy bowl.

Steamed Chicken

2 young Chickens
1 Lemon
5 large slices Larding
    Pork (thin)
3 small Carrots
3 small Parsnips
10 small White Onions
3 stalks Celery
6 small round Potatoes
½ tsp. Paprika
Salt — Pepper
Stock
½ cup Cream
1 Egg Yolk

Select 2 young Chickens 2½ pounds each. Cut leg and second joint apart, and each breast in two pieces. Skin and rub with lemon. Boil skin, giblet, heart and bones in small amount of water, 1 tbsp. salt, 1 bay leaf and four allspice one hour. Line a large casserole with larding pork. Place chicken in middle. Cut carrots and parsnips with a fluted knife ½ inch crossways. Leave small white onions and potatoes whole. Cut celery in squares. Place vegetables in separate mounds around the meat. Pour chicken broth over. Sprinkle with paprika, salt and pepper. Cover dish, put in oven and bake until vegetables are ready. If necessary, add a little more broth while cooking. Just before serving, mix cream with egg yolk and pour over all, turning the dish so as to distribute cream evenly. Heat but do not boil. Sprinkle with chopped parsley. Serve hot in same dish.

Squab Chicken—Swedish Style—(Persilje-Kyckling)

4 Squab Chickens
½ cup Butter
1 cup Cream
½ cup Chopped Parsley
1 tbsp. Flour
Salt and Pepper

Clean and dry chickens. Saute livers, chop and mix with chopped parsley in half of butter, salt and pepper. Stuff chickens and tie with string. Brown in Dutch oven, baste with broth and simmer from 20 to 30 minutes. Remove chickens and keep hot. Sprinkle flour into stock, add cream and season well. Cook gravy few minutes and strain. Serve with "Lingon" (Swedish cranberries) and cucumbers (Swedish style). Boil neck, feet, wing tips and giblets for broth.

Fried Chicken (Scandia)

2 Broilers 2 lb. each
8 slices Bacon
½ cup Chopped Parsley
2 cups Broth
1 cup Cream
4 Allspice
½ lb. mushrooms
1 Onion
1 Small Carrot
2 stalks Celery
Salt — Pepper — Paprika
½ cup Flour
1 cup Bread Crumbs

Cut off wings at second joint, also legs above the first knuckle. Skin the whole chicken and tear carefully wing and meat from bones, leaving leg and second joint whole, making four pieces of each broiler. Clean and boil skin, giblet and bones with seasoning and vegetables for broth. Fry bacon and keep crisp. Mix flour, crumbs, salt, pepper, paprika and dip chicken in same. Brown in bacon fat and part butter if needed. Place fowl in oven not too hot, 10 to 15 minutes. Make gravy in same frying pan, using flour mixture, broth and cream. Strain, add parsley and sliced sauteed mushroom. Arrange chicken and bacon on platter, pour gravy around or serve separate. Serve with "Swedish Lingon."

Chicken Croquettes

2 cups Minced Cooked
    Chicken
1 cup Cream Sauce
½ cup Chopped Olives
1 tbsp. Escoffier Sauce
2 Eggs
½ cup Flour
1 cup Bread Crumbs
Salt — Pepper

Mix chicken with cream sauce, olives and escoffier sauce. Salt and pepper to taste. Add 1 egg-yolk. Do not boil. Fold in stiffly beaten eggwhite last. Cool, and shape into cones. Roll in flour, then in beaten egg, and last in bread crumbs. Fry in deep fat (preferably oil). Serve hot with Foam Sauce.

Chicken Croquettes with Rice

1 cup Minced Cooked
    Chicken
1 cup Boiled Rice
1 cup Thick Cream Sauce
½ cup Chopped Green
    Pepper
1 tbsp. Chutney Sauce
2 Eggs

Prepare same as Chicken Croquettes using half rice.

Potted Chicken

2 Broilers (2½ lbs. each)
1 cup finely cut Bacon
    or Ham
2 tbsp. chopped Green
    Pepper
2 tbsp. chopped Pimento
1 cup soft white Bread
    crumbs
1 Egg
Stock, Milk, Cream
Salt — Pepper

Clean broilers as usual. Cut chicken in eight pieces, two legs, two second joints, and each breast in two. Put neck, feet, heart, gizzard and breastbone in same pan. Cover with water and boil one hour or more, liver only five minutes. Roll chicken in flour, mixed with one tbsp. salt and one fourth tsp. pepper, dip in beaten eggs and lastly in bread crumbs. Fry in deep fat or frying pan to light brown color. Arrange layer of chicken in baking dish, sprinkle with ham or bacon, chopped liver, green pepper, pimento, and salt to taste, then proceed with another layer of meat till all is used. Strain about two cups of chicken broth over cover and let simmer slowly one hour. Just before serving add one cup of cream, let come to a boil and serve in same dish.

Chicken Souffle

2 cups Minced Cooked
    Chicken
2 cups Cream Sauce
2 Eggs
1 tsp. Escoffier Sauce
Salt — Pepper

Mix chicken with hot cream sauce. Add egg-yolks but do not boil. Last, fold in stiffly beaten eggwhites. Pour into a well buttered baking dish. Place dish in pan of hot water and bake in moderate oven for 30 minutes. (Chicken Souffle may be prepared with half amount of chicken and half amount of sauted mushrooms, or boiled rice.)

Chicken Croquettes with Mushrooms

2 cup Minced Cooked
    Chicken
½ lb. Sauted Mushrooms
    coursely chopped
2 cups Cream Sauce
2 Eggs

Prepare same as Chicken Croquettes using half mushrooms.

Chicken and Nut Balls

1 cup Minced Cooked
    Chicken
1 cup Rich Cream Sauce
½ cup Crushed Peanuts
    or Pecan
1 tbsp. Chopped Parsley
1 Egg
Few grains Cayenne
Pinch of Paprika
Salt — Pepper
Flour and Bread Crumbs

Mix chicken with nuts, parsley, cayenne, paprika, salt and pepper to taste. Add to cream sauce and heat thoroughly. Add egg-yolk—but do not boil. Cool. Shape into small balls and roll in flour, then in eggwhite and, last, in soft white bread crumbs. Fry to golden color in deep fat (preferably oil). If desired, serve with Foam Sauce.

Chicken Livers with Mushrooms

1 cup Chicken Livers
2 cups Button Mushrooms
1 tbsp. Flour
1 cup Cream or rich Milk
3 tbsp. Sherry
Butter
Salt — Pepper

Saute diced livers, mushroom caps and chopped stems. Sprinkle with flour; add cream and seasoning. Simmer 5 minutes. Add Sherry. Heat.

Chicken Stew-Soup

1 Fowl 4½ to 5 pounds
2 Bay Leaves
6 Allspice
1 tsp. Salt
1½ cup each, carrots,
    Parsnips, Celery
1 cup Small White Onions
1 cup Tiny Potatoes
1 cup Cubed Firm
    Tomatoes
½ cup Leek
1 tbsp. Green Pepper
1 tbsp. Parsley (chopped)

Clean and wash fowl. Remove all fat and melt for frying. Use livers for other dishes. Cut feet and neck off; wash and boil with whole chicken, also giblet and heart. Cover chicken with water, add salt and let it come to a boil. Skim. Add bay leaf and allspice. Let simmer until breast is done. Cut breast from bird and put the rest back in soup. Add the nicely cut vegetables except parsley. Boil about 25 to 30 minutes. Take out meat, discard bones. Cut all meat in inch squares. Reheat in soup; add parsley and serve hot on deep dinner plates.

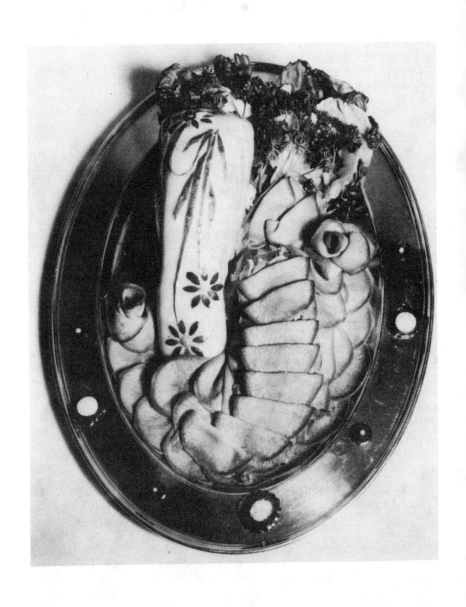

Smoked Beef Tongue

Game and Poultry

Connoisseurs do of course enjoy Game of all kinds, as they have cultivated their tastes in culinary art, and the discovery of a new blending of ingredients never fails to evoke their interest.

●

Many rare dishes have originated purely by accident. Discovery of the fact that Game gained in flavor by hanging a few days before cooking was hailed by the connoisseurs.

Roast Pheasant "Stekt Fasan"   Fried Partridge "Stekta Rapphöns"

Quail "Vaktel"   Roast Reindeer No. 1 "Renstek"

Braised Black Grouse "Stekt Orre"   Roast Reindeer No. 2 "Renstek"

Ragout of Duck

Roast Pheasant (Stekt Fasan)

Pheasant should hang at least two weeks in a cold place before being plucked, cleaned, and roasted.

Rub bird with lemon, then with salt, pepper and sugar. Cover breast with a slice of larding-pork, bind together with string, and brown in oven, basting every few minutes with a good stock or with hot milk. A young pheasant requires about 40 to 50 minutes roasting, but older birds take longer to become tender. Remove string and pork and make a rather thick gravy of flour and cream in roasting pan. If desired, the bird may be stuffed with chestnut, mushrooms, or any other good stuffing. Serve with wine jelly.

When pheasants are served on buffet or "Smörgåsbord" their beautiful plumage is carefully removed and used as a decoration. The feathers are placed in natural position and the birds are carved at the table.

Quail (Vaktel)

This is one of the few wild birds which should be cooked soon after killing. Pluck, singe, clean and wipe the birds with a damp cloth. Rub the inside with salt and cover the breast with a thin slice of larding-pork, then bind and truss into shape. Broil or roast about 10 to 15 minutes. Place birds on pieces of buttered toast and garnish with lemon. If preferred, the birds may be fried in butter. About 30 minutes is required for frying and when done, remove the strings and pork. Cut the quail in half lengthwise and place in a deep dish or casserole. Pour over any juice that is in the pan and serve.

Braised Black Grouse (Stekt Orre)

Pluck, singe, clean and wash the grouse hens. Salt thin slices of larding-pork and lay between the skin and breast meat. Sew the skin and truss the hens into shape. Brown in butter on all sides and baste with some stock and cream. Braise slowly until tender (about 1½ hours for young hens) basting often with stock and cream or rich milk. Make a gravy from the pan juice in the usual way and add a teaspoonful of black currant jelly.

Fried Partridge (Stekta Rapphöns)

Pluck, singe, clean and wipe the birds. Sew skin together and cover breasts with a thin slice of larding-pork. Bind and truss into shape and brown birds in butter. Sprinkle with salt and fry for about half an hour, or until tender. Baste with rich milk or cream. When serving, remove strings and larding-pork and cut in half lengthwise. Pour pan juice over birds or make a rich gravy to be served separately. Garnish the platter with small pieces of toast which have been spread with a mixture consisting of the cooked livers ground or chopped very fine, seasoned, and flavored with a little Madeira wine.

Roast Reindeer No. 1 (Renstek)

8 lb. Leg of Deer
4 quarts Milk
½ lb. Larding-Pork
1 tbsp. Salt
1 tsp. Celery Salt
¼ tsp. Pepper
2 cups rich Milk
2 cups Stock or Water
1 cup Cream
2 tbsp. Flour
Butter or Fat

Soak meat in milk for a few hours or over night. Cut pork in strips. Dip in mixed salt, celery salt, and pepper, and with a larding needle, place in rows through the meat. Rub meat with rest of salt mixture. Brown in fat on all sides. Baste alternately with stock (or water) and hot milk and roast under cover slowly for 2 or 3 hours or until meat is well done. Remove to serving platter. Add flour and cream to pan juice and cook a few minutes. Strain and serve separately. Serve sweet-sour relish and jelly with hot or cold meat.

Roast Reindeer No. 2 (Renstek)

6 to 8 lb. Leg of Deer
1 Onion
1 Carrot
2 Bay Leaves
6 Whole Allspice
6 Whole White Pepper
1 tsp. Ginger
1 tsp. Celery Salt
1 tbsp. Salt
1 tbsp. Sugar
¼ tsp. Pepper
1 Lemon (sliced fine)
2 cups White Wine
1 cup Stock or Water
1 cup Cream
2 Eggs
1 cup Oil

Trim meat and wipe with wet towel. Mix salt, pepper, ginger, celery salt together and rub well into meat. Brown in oil on all sides. Add all other ingredients except eggs and cream. Cover roasting pot and simmer slowly 2½ hours or until meat is well done. Turn meat every 15 minutes. When done, remove to a platter. Pour cream in roasting pan and boil one minute. Strain into a small sauce pan and just before serving, beat 2 egg yolks into gravy. Heat until gravy thickens but do not boil. Fold in stiffly beaten whites and serve. Raw cranberry relish, fine wine jelly, watermelon rind or some other good relish should be served with this roast.

Ragout of Duck

2 cups left-over Duck Meat
6 Prunes
1 chopped Apple
Stock (from duck bones)
2 tbsp. Butter
1 tbsp. Flour

Boil duck bones with one onion, one carrot, one or two stalks of celery, one bay leaf, six allspice and salt. Soak prunes over night or par boil them. Pit prunes and cut in small pieces. Peel, core and chop apple. Make a thick gravy from butter, flour and strained stock. Add all ingredients, heat thoroughly and serve hot.

Hot Egg Dishes

Hints and Suggestions

Scrambled Eggs make a nutritious, tasty, and easily prepared meal.

Use strictly fresh eggs. To each egg add 1 to 2 tbsp. of liquid—such as water, milk, cream, or stock. Do not overcook eggs as they will become dry. Use very little salt as it has a tendency to make eggs heavy. Melt butter—do not brown, and cook eggs on slow fire, stirring at intervals. Serve immediately when ready.

Instead of poaching eggs in water, use small amount of lightly salted milk. A little melted butter or cheese makes the eggs rich and tasty.

Scrambled Eggs—Swedish Style "Äggstanning"

Plain Scrambled Eggs

Spanish Scrambled Eggs

Scrambled Eggs with Ham on Toast

Scrambled Eggs with Ham and Corn Flakes

Scrambled Eggs with Rice and Bacon

Scrambled Eggs with Ham on English Muffins

Scrambled Eggs with Tomatoes and Ham

Scrambled Eggs with Chicken

Scrambled Eggs with Chives and Sausages

Creamed Eggs and Bacon

Poached Eggs with Ham and Hollandaise Sauce

Eggs with Spinach and Cheese

Poached Eggs with Fish

Eggs with Summer Sausage (Medwurst)

Eggs with Mushroom Sauce

Custard with Cheese Sauce

Scrambled Eggs—Swedish Style (Äggstanning)

4 Eggs
1 cup Rich Milk
3 tbsp. Butter
1 tsp. Sugar
Salt — Pepper

Whip eggs and milk together with sugar, salt and pepper. Melt butter in top part of double-boiler and pour in mixture. Place pan in boiling water; lower flame and keep water at boiling point until set. (If water is briskly boiling, the eggs become watery.) Serve plain or with ham. bacon, or sausages, as desired. Cubed chicken, chicken liver, minced ham or tongue or picked fish may be mixed with eggs and cooked. This is a very easy and practical way to prepare scrambled eggs as it requires little attention and eggs can not scorch or bake in buttered dish placed in water in moderate oven.

Plain Scrambled Eggs

4 Eggs
3 tbsp. Butter
6 tbsp. Liquid (Water, Milk, Cream)
Pinch of Sugar
Few grains Salt
Dash of Pepper

Beat eggs with a fork. Add liquid, sugar, salt and pepper. Melt butter in skillet and add egg mixture. Move mixture with spatula towards handle of skillet. When set, but yet soft, remove to hot platter.

Spanish Scrambled Eggs

6 Eggs
1 cup Pepper Pot Soup
1 cup Canned Tomatoes
1 tsp. Sugar

Boil tomatoes in skillet 5 minutes. Add Pepper Pot Soup and let come to a boil. Add sugar, also salt and pepper if needed. Then add eggs and scramble.

Scrambled Eggs with Ham on Toast

4 Eggs Scrambled
4 slices Toast
4 slices Ham

Place a thin slice of broiled ham on toast. Top with scrambled eggs.

Scrambled Eggs with Ham and Corn Flakes

6 Eggs, Scrambled
1½ cups Corn Flakes
6 slices Ham

Heap eggs on middle of platter. Place ham at each end and heated corn flakes on both sides.

Scrambled Eggs with Rice and Bacon

12 slices Bacon
½ cup Milk
6 Eggs
½ cup Rice (raw)
½ cup Butter
1 tbsp. Sugar
Salt — Pepper
1 tbsp. Chopped Parsley

Boil rice in plenty of water for 15 minutes. Strain, and pour hot water over rice in strainer to wash off starch. Put rice in double boiler with half of butter; add sugar, salt and pepper. Cook rice until tender, but not too soft. When ready, fill rice into buttered cone-shaped mold. Scramble eggs in remaining butter. Turn out rice cone onto middle of serving platter, and surround with the scrambled eggs. Broil bacon crisp and stand up against the rice cone. Sprinkle with parsley and serve.

Scrambled Eggs with Ham on English Muffins

4 Eggs, Scrambled
2 English Muffins
4 tbsp. Chopped Ham
4 tsp. Parmesan Cheese
   (grated)
Butter
Salt — Pepper

Split English muffins. Toast and butter. Cover with chopped ham and top with scrambled eggs. Then cover with grated cheese and brown quickly under broiler.

Scrambled Eggs with Tomatoes and Ham

4 Eggs
8 tbsp. Water
4 slices Ham
4 slices Tomato
4 slices Toast (Whole
   Wheat Bread)
2 tbsp. Butter
Salt — Pepper

Scramble eggs. Place on toast, then add medium thick slice of fried ham. Top with slices of tomato previously dipped in flour and fried in ham fat. Or, place ham on toast, then tomatoes, and top with eggs. Sprinkle with parsley.

Scrambled Eggs with Chicken

4 Eggs
½ cup Finely Cut Chicken
6 tbsp. Chicken Broth or
   Cream
4 slices White Bread
6 tbsp. Butter
1 tbsp. Chopped Parsley
Salt — Pepper

Mix chicken with eggs, broth, or cream. Season well, and scramble. Toast bread on one side and fry the other side in butter. Cover toast with egg mixture. Sprinkle with parsley.

Scrambled Eggs with Chives and Sausages

4 Eggs
8 tbsp. Rich Milk
2 tsp. Finely Cut Chives
2 tbsp. Butter
½ lb. Pork Sausages
Salt — Pepper

Add mixed chives to beaten eggs and milk. Scramble. Serve with broiled pork sausages.

Creamed Eggs and Bacon

6 Eggs (Hard-Boiled)
1 cup Rich Cream Sauce
1½ cups Grapenuts
    (Heated)
12 slices Bacon
1 tbsp. Chopped Parsley
Salt — Pepper

Cut and mix eggwhites with rich cream sauce. Season well. Place on serving dish. Top with egg-yolks squeezed through potato ricer. Sprinkle with finely chopped parsley. Make border of heated grapenuts. (Pieces of toast may be used instead of grapenuts.) Arrange strips of crisp bacon on top of eggs.

Poached Eggs with Ham and Hollandaise Sauce

4 Eggs
2 English Muffins
4 slices Ham
1 cup Hollandaise Sauce
1 tbsp. Chopped Truffles

Split English muffins. Toast and butter. On each half muffin place a slice of broiled ham. Top with poached egg and cover with Hollandaise sauce. Sprinkle with chopped truffles. (Toast may be used instead of muffins.)

Eggs with Spinach and Cheese

6 Eggs
1 lb. Spinach
6 pcs. Toast (Round)
1 cup Cream Sauce
⅔ cup Grated Cheese
3 tbsp. Butter
Salt — Pepper

Steam spinach 10 minutes. Drain. Heat in butter and season well. Cover toast with spinach. Top with poached egg and cover with cream sauce. Sprinkle with grated cheese. Brown under broiler.

Poached Eggs with Fish

6 Eggs
3 English Muffins
1 cup Tuna Fish
1½ cups Cream Sauce
½ cup Grated Cheese
Butter
Dash of Tabasco
Salt — Pepper

Mix fish with cream sauce. Add seasoning. Split muffins; toast and butter. Cover muffin halves with creamed fish, and top with poached egg. Sprinkle with cheese and brown in very hot oven or under broiler.

Eggs with Summer Sausage (Medwurst)

6 large slices of Summer Sausage
3 Eggs
6 tbsp. Cream
1 tbsp. Chopped Parsley
Cornflakes or Toast
Salt — Pepper

Fry sausages on one side, leaving skin on to make them cup-shaped. Scramble egg mixture with parsley and season well. Fill sausage cups and serve on a bed of heated cornflakes or round pieces of toast.

Eggs with Mushroom Sauce

6 Eggs
1 lb. Mushrooms
1 cup Milk
1 cup Cream
1 tbsp. Flour
⅓ cup Butter
Salt — Pepper
Sherry (optional)

Select medium sized mushrooms. Pick out 12 even sized caps and saute in butter. Keep warm. If stems are not woody, chop and use with remaining sliced caps. Simmer in butter ten to fifteen minutes. Sprinkle with flour, add milk and let boil three minutes. Boil eggs six or seven minutes. Peel, cut in half, crossways; place on small round pieces of toast on hot platter; add cream to mushrooms, pour around eggs and put mushroom caps on eggs. Serve hot. Add 3 tablespoons of Sherry to sauce if preferred.

Custard with Cheese Sauce

6 Eggs
1 qt. heated Milk
1 tsp. Salt
½ tsp. Celery Salt
Dash Pepper

Cheese Sauce
3 tbsp. Butter
2 tbsp. Flour
2 cups Milk
1 tsp. Dry Mustard
1 tsp. Sugar
Dash Cayenne
½ lb. grated American Cheese

Beat eggs in a bowl and season with salt, celery salt and pepper. Add warm milk, mix well and pour mixture in a well buttered ring mold. Bake in a pan of hot water over a low flame or in a slow oven about half an hour until custard is set. Unmold and serve with Cheese Sauce and Melba toast. Cheese Sauce: Melt butter, add flour, milk and seasoning and cook for a few minutes. Add grated cheese and keep warm over boiling water. Stir sauce until well blended.

Note: Any kind of grated cheese may be used for this sauce. Season accordingly.

Omelettes

Hints and Suggestions

Omelettes are very helpful in case of unexpected guests. There are always ingredients on hand for a savory and palatable omelette, such as eggs, cream or milk, and some kind of left-over meat, vegetables, or jam. It requires practice to make a fine omelette, but it is worth the effort.

Omelettes must not be over-cooked, as we so often find them; they become dry, heavy, and tough. The heavy frying pan is best for rolled or folded omelettes, as the butter must be sizzling when the eggs are poured in; afterward, shake skillet and lower flame to about medium. As soon as the edge of omelette stiffens (eggs still soft on top) roll or fold omelette and turn out on serving platter. When using filling for omelettes, place one-third of the filling inside the omelette before folding, and pour the remainder on the side or around the omelette. Serve at once.

French Omelette	Ham or Bacon Omelette
Fluffy Omelette	Lobster Omelette
Omelette with Flour	Crabmeat Omelette
Boiled Omelette	Shrimp Omelette
Chicken Omelette No. 1	Omelette with Tomatoes
Chicken Omelette No. 2	Omelette with Tomato Sauce
Chicken Liver Omelette	Mushroom Omelette
Omelette with Liverwurst	Asparagus Tip Omelette
Omelette No. 1 with Tongue	Pineapple Omelette
Omelette No. 2 with Tongue	Strawberry Omelette

French Omelette

4 Eggs
4 tbsp. Cream
4 tbsp. Water
3 tbsp. Butter
(If butter is salted, no extra seasoning is necessary)

Beat whole eggs with a fork, adding cream and water. Melt butter in heavy frying pan until sizzling. Pour eggs into pan and when edge becomes firm, but mixture is still soft on top, add ⅓ filling before folding (see hints and suggestions). Turn on hot platter, and pour remainder of filling on side or around omelette. Serve immediately.

This omelette may be filled with meat, fish, vegetables, fruit, jam or jelly.

Fluffy Omelette

4 Eggs
4 tbsp. Cream
4 tbsp. Butter
Seasoning

Beat egg-yolks until lemon colored. Mix in cream and fold in stiffly beaten eggwhites. Melt butter in frying pan until sizzling hot and pour in egg mixture. Fry until golden brown on bottom; then slightly brown top of omelette under broiler. Pour creamed fish, meat, or vegetables on platter and cover with omelette, or pour filling on half and fold other half over. Serve at once.

Omelette with Flour

2 Eggs
1 tsp. Flour
½ cup Milk
2 tbsp. Butter
Seasoning

Beat egg-yolks, flour, milk and seasoning (salt and pepper) together. Fold in stiffly beaten whites. Pour into hot buttered frying pan. Move mixture with spatula and let brown nicely. Add desired filling and turn on hot serving platter. For economy, this omelette may be used with very good results.

Boiled Omelette

3 cups Milk
3 tbsp. Flour
3 Eggs
½ cup Butter
1 tsp. Sugar
1 tsp. Salt
Pinch of Pepper

Melt butter. Add flour, sugar, and salt. Add hot milk and boil, beating vigorously until the batter loosens from the pan. Remove from stove and beat in 1 egg-yolk at a time. Fold in stiffly beaten eggwhites. Pour into well buttered omelette pan and bake in oven until golden brown. This omelette will not fall as easily as omelettes without flour, and it is practical for meat or fish fillings.

NOTE: The preceding 4 recipes can be used for the omelette proper or for foundation of any of the following fillings. (Use salt very sparingly in the omelette proper as it tends to make the omelette heavy.)

Chicken Omelette No. 1

1 cup Minced Chicken
1½ cups Cream Sauce or
    Chicken Gravy
Paprika
Salt
Pepper

Add minced chicken to cream sauce or chicken gravy. Season well. Fold ⅓ filling in omelette, and pour remainder on side.

Chicken Omelette No. 2

1 cup Minced Chicken
1 tbsp. Parsley, Chopped
Salt — Pepper
1 cup Milk or Broth

Heat minced chicken in broth or cream. Strain. Distribute chicken and parsley evenly on omelette before folding.

Chicken Liver Omelette

½ cup Chicken Livers
    sauted and minced
½ cup Celery, Chopped
1 cup Cream Sauce
Salt and Pepper to taste

Boil chopped celery 5 minutes. Strain Add chicken livers and celery to cream sauce. Season well. Fold filling in omelette.

Omelette with Liverwurst

¼ lb. Liverwurst
6 Chopped Olives
Salt — Pepper

Press liverwurst through potato ricer and distribute all over omelette while cooking. Sprinkle with chopped olives (squeezed dry in towel) before folding omelette.

Omelette No. 1 with Tongue

4 slices Tongue, Boiled
Pinch Paprika

Slice tongue into tiny strips and distribute over omelette before folding. Add a dash of paprika.

Omelette No. 2 with Tongue

1 cup Boiled Ox Tongue
    (cut in strips)
1 small can Tomato Soup
⅓ cup Green Pepper
Few grains Cayenne

Cook green pepper in tomato soup 5 minutes. Add tongue and cayenne. Fold ⅓ filling in omelette, and pour remainder on side.

Ham or Bacon Omelette

2 tbsp. Minced Ham or
    Bacon
1 tbsp. Butter
Pinch of Pepper

Simmer minced ham or bacon in skillet for 2 or 3 minutes. (Remove part of fat if there is too much.) Add omelette mixture and carefully shake until almost settled. Fold.

Lobster Omelette

1 cup Lobster, Fresh Boiled
    or Canned
½ cup Milk
1 Egg
2 tbsp. Sherry
½ cup Cream
Pinch of Sugar
Salt — Pepper

Heat cubed lobster in milk and cream. Add egg-yolk and shake mixture, but do not boil. Season to taste. Add sherry. Last, add stiffly beaten egg-white. Fold in omelette.

Crabmeat Omelette

1 cup Crabmeat, Cooked
1 cup Shredded Celery
1 cup Rich Milk
1 Egg
Pinch Cayenne
Salt — Pepper

Saute celery in butter from 7 to 10 minutes. Add crabmeat, milk, cayenne, salt and pepper to taste. When well heated, add egg-yolk mixed with a tbsp. milk or water. Heat mixture, but do not boil. Fold in stiffly beaten eggwhite. Place mixture in omelette before folding.

Shrimp Omelette

1 lb. Fresh Shrimp
Dill and Salt
2 cups Tomato Soup
Dash of Tabasco
Salt — Pepper

Plunge fresh shrimp in boiling water with salt and few sprays of dill. Boil 15 minutes. Shell and cut shrimp in 3 or 4 pieces and boil a few minutes in tomato soup. Add tabasco, 1 tbsp. chopped fresh dill, salt and pepper to taste. Fold ⅓ filling in omelette, and pour remainder on side.

Omelette with Tomatoes

3 Tomatoes
½ cup Flour
1 tsp. Sugar
1 tsp. Salt
Pinch of Pepper

Cut thin slice off each end of tomato and make two slices of remaining part. Dip in flour mixed with sugar, salt and pepper. Fry in butter. Place around omelette.

Omelette with Tomato Sauce

1 can Tomatoes
1 Bay Leaf
4 Allspice
1 tbsp. Sugar
½ cup Chopped Onions
1 tsp. Salt
Pinch of Pepper
4 tbsp. Butter

Saute onions 5 minutes. Add all ingredients. Cook slowly 20 minutes. Strain, and pour around omelette.

Mushroom Omelette

1 cup Mushrooms, Sliced
2 tbsp. Butter
1 tbsp. Flour
1 cup Rich Milk
Pinch of Paprika
Salt — Pepper

Saute mushrooms in butter 5 minutes. Add flour, milk, and seasoning. Fold 1/3 filling omelette, and pour remainder on side.

Asparagus Tip Omelette

1 can Asparagus Tips
2 tbsp. Butter
1 tbsp. Flour
1 tbsp. Chutney Sauce
Cream
Salt — Pepper

Heat asparagus tips in own liquid. Make a sauce of butter, flour, liquid from asparagus, and add enough cream to make the sauce medium thick. Season. Cut half of asparagus tips in two or three pieces, mix in sauce and fill in omelette. Garnish with remaining tips, or place asparagus on ends of platter and pour sauce over.

Pineapple Omelette

1 can Crushed Pineapple
4 tbsp. Pineapple Juice
4 tbsp. Butter

Strain pineapple. Mix pineapple juice with well beaten egg-yolks. Fold in stiffly beaten egg-whites. Pour into hot butter in a wide frying pan and slightly brown. When set, place pan under broiler to lightly brown top. Spread pineapple pulp, warm, on top of omelette. Fold carefully and serve immediately.

Strawberry Omelette

4 tbsp. Butter
1/2 cup Cream
2 cups Strawberries
1/3 cup Sugar
1/2 cup Sherry
2 tbsp. Liqueur (any good brand)

Stem, wash, and crush strawberries. Mix sugar, sherry, and liqueur, and pour over berries. Let stand one hour. Prepare omelette proper same as Pineapple Omelette, using cream instead of pineapple juice. Heat strawberries by placing saucepan or bowl in hot water. Fill in and around omelette.

NOTE: Any good fruit may be prepared and used with omelettes as above.

Pancakes, etc.

Hints and Suggestions

With Swedish pancakes "Plättar," it is customary to use imported Swedish "Lingon" (wild cranberries). Any jam or berries may be substituted.

Swedish "Plättpanna" (individual sectional griddle) may be purchased in most of the large department stores. The griddle is so designed that seven separate cakes may be made at one time. They are quite small and generally seven cakes are used as a portion. Always try the batter with one cake. If edges turns upward add a little more milk until you get the right consistency. Some kinds of flour swell more than others. Eggs also differ.

Pancake Batter No. I

Pancake Batter without Eggs No. 2

Pancakes with Chicken

Pork or Bacon Pancakes "Fläsk Pannkaka"

Pancakes with Pate de Foie Gras

Pancakes with Liverwurst

Pancakes with Ham

Pancakes with Vegetables

Swedish Pancakes "Plättar"

Fruit Pancakes "Frukt Plättar"

Layer Pancakes

Apple Pancakes "Äppel Plättar"

French Pancakes "Crepe Suzette"

Corn Pancakes

Pancake Batter No. 1

3 Eggs
1 cup Flour
3 cups Milk
2 tbsp. Sugar
½ tsp. Salt
Butter

Beat yolks with egg beater. Gradually add milk, sifted flour, sugar and salt. Beat until batter is very smooth. Let stand 2 or 3 hours. When needed, fold in stiffly beaten egg whites and fry in heavy pan or on griddle. The pan must be sizzling hot and the butter slightly brown for tender cakes. If rich cakes are desired, use part cream instead of milk, or add melted butter to batter. Whipped cream also makes the batter light.

Pancake Batter without Eggs No. 2

1 cup Cream
1 cup Flour
Salt and Sugar
Butter for frying

Whip cream. Fold in sifted flour. Season with salt and sugar to taste. Fry on hot griddle on one side only. Roll, and serve at once.

Pancakes with Chicken

1 cup Cooked Chicken
1 cup Thin Cream Sauce

Cut chicken fine and mix with cream sauce. Fry pancake batter No. 1 on griddle. Spread with creamed chicken. Roll, and serve hot.

Pork or Bacon Pancakes (Fläsk Pannkaka)

4 Eggs
1 qt. Milk
6 slices Salt Pork or Bacon
1 tsp. Sugar
½ cup Flour
Pepper

Beat yolks until light. Add flour and milk alternately, which will make batter smooth. Fold in stiffly beaten whites. Pour batter over fried pork and bake in hot oven for 10 minutes. Reduce heat and finish baking until mixture is set in center (or about 10 to 20 minutes). (If there is too much fat from pork, pour off part.)

Pancakes with Pate de Foie Gras

Pate de Foie Gras
Cream

Mix Pate de Foie Gras with cream until it spread easily. Fry pancakes No. 1 and spread with thin mixture. Roll, and serve hot. If preferred, stack seven cakes with mixture between each layer. Keep hot. Cut like cake at table and serve.

Pancakes with Liverwurst

Liverwurst
Cream

Follow recipe for Pancakes with Pate de Foie Gras, substituting liverwurst.

Pancakes with Ham

Cooked Ham
Cream or Mayonnaise

Grind ham fine and mix with cream or mayonnaise until it spreads easily. Slightly heat mixture. Spread on hot cakes and serve.

Pancakes with Vegetables

Cubed Vegetables
(Cooked)

Cube cooked vegetables—such as celery, carrots, parsnips, etc. Vegetables may be mixed with batter or sprinkled on pancakes. It is preferable to use batter without eggs. Fold vegetables in cakes and serve.

Swedish Pancakes (Plättar)

2 Eggs
2 cups Rich Milk
   or more
1 tbsp. Sugar
2 heaping tbsp. Flour
3 tbsp. Melted Butter
Pinch of Salt

Beat well the 2 egg yolks. Add alternately flour and milk. Stir in sugar, salt, and melted butter. Make batter preferably a few hours before required. Fold in stiffly beaten egg whites. When butter is used in batter, very little is required for frying.

Apple Pancakes (Äppel plättar)

Swedish Pancake Batter
Apples
Syrup

Pare, core, and slice apples. Cook in plain syrup for 2 or 3 minutes. Drain. Proceed as in Swedish Pancakes. Fill griddle sections half full of batter, and place 1 slice of apple in each section. (Griddle should be sizzling hot.) Brown on both sides. Sprinkle with sugar.

Fruit Pancake (Frukt plättar)

Swedish Pancake Batter
Jam, Jelly, or Applesauce

Proceed as in Swedish Pancakes. Spread jam, jelly, or applesauce on one side of cakes and fold in half-moon shape. Arrange on hot platter and serve immediately.

97

Layer Pancakes

Pancake Batter No. 1
Jam or Mashed Fruit
Whipped Cream

Proceed as in Pancake Batter No. 1. On a round platter, stack one pancake on top of the other, spreading each one with jam or mashed fruit. Seven or eight thin layers is a desired height. Keep warm over hot water with cover on cakes. Just before serving, pour whipped cream over cakes. Cut like a layer cake and serve.

French Pancakes (Crepe Suyette)

3 Eggs
1 cup Flour
1 cup Milk
1 cup Cream
Butter
1 tbsp. Sugar
2 Glass Bar-le-Duc
1 cup Orange Juice
4 tbsp. Brandy
4 tbsp. Liqueur

Beat egg-yolks. Add alternately flour, milk, and cream. Stir in sugar, salt, and melted butter. Batter should be made a few hours before required. When ready to use, fold in stiffly beaten eggwhites. Fry pancakes about 6 inches in diameter. Spread cakes with Bar-le-Duc. Roll and place in chafing dish or on hot platter. Mix orange juice, brandy, and liqueur (Curacao, Grand Marnier, or Benedictine warm and pour over pancakes. Sprinkle with sugar, touch a match to sauce and baste pancakes while burning. One must be careful lighting the dish as one might get scared, and upset the dish and burn oneself. Don't burn liqueur too long as it loses its flavor.

Corn Pancakes

2 Eggs
½ cup Flour
1 cup Grated Corn
3 cups Milk
1 tsp. Salt
Dash of Pepper

Beat eggs, flour, milk and corn gradually to a smooth batter. Let stand one or two hours to swell. Make small cakes on griddle or in a Swedish "Plättpanna". Serve plain or with bacon, country sausages, or broiled ham.

Make small cakes, wrap a broiled or baked cocktail sausage in each one and serve hot.

Roll corn pancakes and place on a hot platter. Sprinkle freely with crushed bacon previously fried crisp.

Make corn pancakes. Put ⅓ teaspoon of corn syrup on half; fold over other half and serve hot.

Stuffed Eggs

Foundation for All Stuffed Eggs

Slowly boil fresh eggs from 7 to 10 minutes (never more than 10 minutes). Shell and cut in half lengthwise with a plain or fluted edged knife. Carefully remove egg-yolks, leaving the whites whole. Squeeze yolks through a potato ricer, or press them through a strainer into a bowl and work in the different seasonings with a wooden spoon. With a pastry bag or spoon fill egg-whites with following recipes:

Plain Stuffed Eggs

Eggs Russe

Eggs Italienne

Eggs with "Sill i Dill"

Eggs with Sardellen

Eggs with Anchovy

Eggs with Lobster

Eggs with Pate de Foie Gras

Eggs with Ox Tongue

Eggs with Celery and Nuts

Eggs with Chives

Eggs with Chicken Liver

Eggs with Hats on

Plain Stuffed Eggs

6 Eggs
½ cup Mayonnaise
1 Green Pepper or Tomato
(or both)
Salt — Pepper

Mix egg yolks with mayonnaise. Salt and pepper to taste. Fill whites, Garnish with tiny strips of green pepper and tomatoes. Serve on small lettuce leaves.

Eggs Russe

6 Eggs
2 oz. Russian Caviar
½ cup Cream
½ cup Cream or less
Salt — Pepper

Fill eggwhites with caviar. Mix yolks with cream, salt and pepper, to a smooth paste. With pastry tube garnish around caviar. Serve on chicory.

Eggs Italienne

6 Eggs
2 tbsp. Italian Tomato
Paste
1 raw Eggwhite
1 tsp. Sugar
1 tsp. Lemon Juice
1 tbsp. Gelatin
Salt — Pepper

Mix egg yolks with tomato paste, sugar, lemon juice, gelatin (previously melted) ; salt and pepper to taste. Last, fold in stiffly beaten eggwhite. With this mixture fill eggwhites evenly. Put the two halves together and wrap in waxpaper to keep in shape. Allow time for gelatin to set. Cut with eggslicer and place two or three slices on romaine leaves. Sprinkle with chopped parsley.

Eggs with "Sill i Dill"

6 Eggs
⅓ can "Sill i Dill"
with juice
⅓ cup Mayonnaise

Mash or press "Sill" with egg-yolks through a potato ricer, fine colander, or strainer. Mix in the juice from can, and add mayonnaise. Fill whites with mixture. Sprinkle with finely chopped dill, and serve on white cabbage leaves.

Eggs with Sardellen

6 Eggs
12 Sardellen
12 Whole Capers
½ cup Mayonnaise
1 tbsp. Chopped Capers
1 tbsp. Tarragon Vinegar
1 tbsp. Sugar

Chop or crush 1 tbsp. of capers very fine and mix with egg-yolks. Add vinegar, sugar, and mayonnaise. Fill eggwhites with mixture through pastry tube. Place sardellen around mixture like a border, and one whole caper on top.

Eggs with Anchovy

6 Eggs
2 tsp. Anchovy Paste (in tube)
½ cup Mayonnaise
1 tsp. Sugar

Mix egg yolks with anchovy paste, sugar, and mayonnaise. Fill eggwhites with mixture. Sprinkle with very fine chopped parsley. Serve on finely shredded red cabbage.

Eggs with Lobster

6 Eggs
1 cup Boiled Lobster freshed or canned
½ cup French Dressing
Dash of Tabasco
2 tbsp. Mayonnaise
Salt — Pepper

Cut lobster in fine cubes. Marinate one hour in French dressing mixed with tabasco sauce. Drain. Mix eggyolks with mayonnaise, salt and pepper, to a stiff paste. Fill eggwhites with lobster. Decorate with mayonnaise through a pastry tube. Serve on escarole.

Eggs with Pate de Foie Gras

6 Eggs
2 oz. Pate de Foie Gras
2 tbsp. Madeira
1 Eggwhite
Few grains Cayenne

Remove truffle from Pate de Foie Gras and use for garnishing. Mix egg-yolks with Pate de Foie Gras to a very smooth paste. Add Madeira (not too cold) drop by drop to paste while stirring. Fold in stiffly beaten white. Fill eggwhites, using a pastry tube. Sprinkle with chopped truffle. Serve on leaves of celery cabbage.

Eggs with Ox Tongue

6 Eggs
¼ lb. Ox Tongue (sliced)
1 cup French Dressing
1 tbsp. Escoffer Sauce
Cream

Cut tongue into fine strips ½ inch long. Marinate in French dressing one hour. Mix egg-yolks with escoffier sauce and enough cream to make a stiff paste. Fill eggwhites with tongue and decorate with paste, using a pastry tube. Place egg halves on tiny lettuce leaves.

Eggs with Celery and Nuts

6 Eggs
⅓ cup Cut Celery
⅓ cup Crushed Walnuts
2 tbsp. Chili Sauce
1 tsp. Sugar
Salt — Pepper

Cut celery into small cubes. Crush walnut meats and mix with egg-yolks. Add chili sauce, salt and pepper. If necessary, soften with mayonnaise. or cream. Fill eggwhites with mixture. Garnish with strips of pimento, tarragon leaves, or green peppers. Decorate platter with celery tops and parsley.

Eggs with Chives

6 Eggs
2 tsp. Fuji Soy Sauce
⅓ cup Finely cut Chives
1 Eggwhite
3 tbsp. Cream
Salt — Pepper

Cut chives fine. (Do not chop.) Mix with egg-yolks, Fuji Soy sauce, cream, salt and pepper to taste. Add chives and fold in stiffly beaten white. Fill eggwhites and serve on shredded lettuce.

Eggs with Chicken Liver

6 Eggs
½ cup Chicken Livers
½ cup Chopped Olives
1 tbsp. Chutney Sauce
2 raw Eggwhites
Salt — Pepper

Saute livers; cool, and mash fine. Add mashed egg-yolks, olives, chutney, salt and pepper to taste. Fold in stiffly beaten eggwhites. Fill eggs with mixture. Decorate with strips of pimento.

Note: Instead of chicken livers, liver-paste or a good liverwurst may be used.

Egg with Hats On

12 small Pullet Eggs
 or 6 regular size
2 or 3 Tomatoes
2 bunches Watercress
 Anchovy paste
12 small round toasts

Boil eggs and shell. If small eggs are available cut one end so they can stand up on bread. If large eggs, cut them in half crossways and place each half on toast spread with mixed butter and anchovy paste. Skin tomatoes, cut a round piece and place like a hat on each egg. Cut bottom stems of cress garnish with green between eggs.

Aspic Dishes and Salads

Aspic Natural

Gelatine or Aspic the Easy Way

Tomato Aspic Ring

Chicken and Walnut Mousse

Salmon Mold

Chicken in Aspic
"A la Daube på Höns"

Pork a la Daube

Meat and Vegetable Aspic

Carrots in Aspic

Salad Mold

Mixed Salad

Colorful Salad Platter

Mixed Green Salad

Decorative Egg Salad

Beet and Egg Salad

Vegetable Salad

Celery Cabbage

Peas and Celery Salad

Cabbage and Pineapple Salad

Vegetable Mold

Cucumber Ring Mold

Shrimps in Aspic

Cabbage, Pineapple and
Carrot Salad

Red Cabbage and Currant Salad

Cabbage, Carrot and Beet Salad

Marmalade and Cabbage Salad

Fruit Marshmallow Mold

Salmon Salad with Vegetables

Caviare and Beet Salad

Kielerspraten and Egg Salad

Potato Salad

Turkey Salad in Cranberry Ring

Tomato and Cheese Ring

Beet Ring

Avocado Salad

Avocado and Grapefruit Salad

Fruit Salad

Romaine and Banana Salad

Banana and Strawberry Salad

Pineapple Salad

Pineapple Fruit Salad

Cottage Cheese and Carrot Mold

Fruit Salad Mold

Shrimp Mold

Alligator Pear Mold

Aspic Natural

4 lbs. Veal Bones
1 cup each Sliced Carrots,
    Parsnips, Leek, Onions
    and Celery
1 Green Pepper
2 Bay Leaves
10 Whole Allspice
3 Egg Whites
2 tbsp. Salt

Cover bones, vegetables and seasoning with cold water. When boiling, skim well. Let simmer 3 to 4 hours. Strain through cheesecloth and cool. If broth is not clear, mix in 2 or 3 egg whites. Place in double boiler and let come to a boil, simmer to clear and strain. (This should make 2 quarts.)

Gelatine or Aspic the Easy Way

There are on the market, various kinds of flavored granulated gelatins which are easy to use for desert and aspic dishes. For buffet service it is especially practical to use these prepared gelatins as they enable one to produce a colorful table at a small cost and with comparatively litttle work involved.

Tomato Aspic Ring

2 tbsp. Gelatine
½ cup Cold Water
1 qt. can Tomatoes
2 Bay Leaves
1 Onion
2 Whole Cloves
1 tbsp. Sugar
1 tsp. Salt
Pinch of Paprika

Soak gelatin in cold water 5 minutes. Boil other ingredients for 30 minutes. Strain. Add gelatin and mix thoroughly. Pour into ring mold and let cool. Place in refrigerator until firm. Invert aspic ring on platter. Fill center with vegetable salad made of cut cooked vegetables — such as carrots, parsnips, string beans, peas, celery, etc., marinated 1 hour in French dressing—or mixed with mayonnaise.

Chicken and Walnut Mousse

3 egg Whites
1 cup Chicken Broth
    or Milk
2 cups of Chicken
    (ground fine)
1½ tsp. gr. Gelatin
⅓ cup Cold Water
1 cup Chopped Walnuts
1 tbsp. Chutney Sauce
1 cup heavy cream
Paprika, Salt, Pepper

Soak gelatin in water as described on package. Add to broth. Add chicken and walnuts, season with chutney, paprika, salt and pepper. Fold in whipped cream and stiffly beaten egg whites. Mold and let set.

Salmon Mold

1½ cup Salmon (flaked)
½ cup Cream
2 tbsp. Gelatine
2 Eggs
1 cup Cream Sauce
Dash Tabasco
Salt and Pepper

Make one cup of cream sauce as usual and add two egg yolks. Season well. When cold, add fish, whipped cream gelatin cooked and last, whipped egg whites. Fill fancy mold. Let set over night. Serve plain or with Foamy Sauce.

Chicken in Aspic (A la Daube på Höns)

Aspic Natural
Cold Chicken, Capon,
    Turkey or Game
Tomatoes
Pimentos
Radishes, etc.
Sliced Eggs
Truffles
Olives

Cover bottom of mold with melted aspic (about ½ inch). When set, add layers of vegetables, truffles, olives, etc., alternated with sliced chicken or other fowl until mold is ¾ filled. Then fill remainder of mold with melted aspic. Cool. Let stand in refrigerator until firm. Turn out on platter. (Instead of aspic one may use gelatin in chicken broths).

Pork a la Daube

2 or 3 lbs. young Pork
    or Pork Filet
1 small Onion
2 Bay Leaves
6 each of Whole Allspice,
    White Pepper and
    Cloves
2 tbsp. Gelatine
Garnishing

Boil pork slowly with salt and spices, about 1½ hours or until meat is cooked, but not too soft to prevent cutting in firm pieces. Dissolve gelatine in ½ cup cold water. Add to broth. Pour part (about 1 inch) in a mold and let set. Garnish with fancy cut cooked vegetables, or tomatoes, radishes, pimentos, etc. Distribute meat on top and strain the almost cool broth on top.

Meat and Vegetable Aspic

2 cups Cooked Cubed Meat
    (Veal, Pork, Chicken
    or Turkey)
2 cups Fancy Cut cooked
    Vegetables
    (Carrots, Parsnips,
    String Beans, Peas
    Celery, etc.)
2 cups Aspic Natural

Place layer of fancy cut vegetables in bottom of mold. Cover with melted aspic, making layer about 1 inch thick. Place in refrigerator. When set, add a layer of cubed meat. Cover with melted aspic and let set. Continue alternating layers of vegetables, aspic, meat, etc., allowing each layer of aspic to set before adding another.

Carrots in Aspic

1 cup Raw Carrots
1 cup Celery
1 package Lime or Lemon
    Jello
Seasoning

Grate raw carrots. Slice Celery crosswise, fine. Mix carrots and celery with dissolved Jello. Season well. Pour into mold and let set. Serve with cold meat.

Salad Mold

1 tbsp. Gelatine
½ cup cold Water
2 cups hot water
1 tbsp. Sugar
1 tsp. Salt
3 tbsp. Lemon Juice
2 cups Cabbage
2 cups Celery
1 Green Pepper
1 Pimento

Soak gelatine a few minutes in cold water. Add sugar, salt, lemon juice and hot water. Cool. Shred cabbage and celery very fine. Chop pimentos coarse. Mix with liquid. Pour into a mold and chill. Turn mold on platter, garnish well and serve ice cold.

Mixed Salad

6 Anchovy Filets
3 boiled Potatoes
3 firm Tomatoes
1 cup Green Peas
2 tsp. Capers
2 Hard-boiled Eggs
½ cup Mayonnaise
½ cup Cream
Salt and Pepper to taste

Cube potatoes, tomatoes and eggs. Add peas, chopped anchovies and capers. Mix with mayonnaise. Whip cream and add to mixture. Chill, and just before serving, mix carefully. Garnish with lettuce, parsley, etc. Serve with cold meat or fish.

Colorful Salad Platter

1 hard White Head of
    Cauliflower
1 cup Carrots
1 cup Parsnips
1 cup Beets
2 cups Peas
French Dressing

Boil cauliflower in salted water with a few slices of lemon and a tablespoon sugar. With a French vegetable cutter make round balls of carrots and parsnips and boil also with salt and sugar cook fresh green peas as usual. Cut balls from cooked beets and do not cook vegetables too much as the appearance and flavor of salad are improved when vegetables are barely soft. Arrange cauliflower in middle of large platter, then alternate the other vegetables in separate mounds around. Pour French dressing over or serve in a bowl.

Mixed Green Salad

1 small Head of Lettuce
½ lb. Endive
1 Spanish Onion
1 bunch Radishes
1 bunch Watercress
2 or 3 hard Red Tomatoes
French Dressing

Break lettuce and endive in one inch pieces. Pick cress from heavy stems, slice radishes thin, skin and cut tomatoes. Slice onion fine. Put all in refrigerator and chill well. Toss together in a bowl and mix with French Dressing.

Decorative Egg Salad

3 Hard-boiled Eggs
4 hard Red Tomatoes (sm.)
1 large Cucumber
1 bunch Watercress
Mayonnaise

Slice Egg with egg slicer — tomatoes and cucumber the same thickness. Make a border of tomatoes, eggs, cucumber, alternating slices, the one overlapping the other. Fill center with watercress from which large stems have been removed.

Beet and Egg Salad

3 Hard-boiled Eggs
6 small Whole Beets
1 crisp Head of Lettuce
Roquefort Dressing

Slice small whole beets with fluted knife in uniform slices. Use egg cutter slicing the eggs. Put crisp lettuce leaves in a salad bowl and arrange slices of beets and eggs among the leaves. Serve dressing separately. Roquefort dressing is made by adding Roquefort cheese to French dressing. Shake well.

Vegetable Salad

1 cup Carrots
1 cup Parsnips
1 cup Celery
1 cup Green Peas
½ cup French Dressing
½ cup Mayonnaise
1 tbsp. Sugar and Salt
Salt and Pepper

Peel and cut carrots, parsnips and celery in even sized pieces. Boil in water with one tablespoon each of salt and sugar. Remove vegetables from fire while still firm and drain. Cook peas separately with soda so they remain green and firm. Chill. Before serving, mix French dressing with mayonnaise. Season if necessary. Pour over salad and serve.

Celery Cabbage

Cut chilled celery cabbage crosswise in one inch pieces and place carefully on slices of skinned raw tomatoes, then a slice of hard boiled egg, and top with half an olive, radish or beet. Pour a spoon of French dressing over each mound and serve on an attractive glass or silver platter.

Peas and Celery Salad

2 cups Green Peas
3 Hard-Boiled Eggs
1 cup Shredded Celery
10 Stuffed Olives (sliced)
1 tbsp. Pimento cut
½ cup Mayonnaise
1 tbsp. Dill (chopped)
1 tbsp. Lemon Juice
1 tsp. Sugar

Cook peas until tender but not soft. Shred celery very fine; cut egg whites and pimentos in strips; slice olives in rings. Chill. Mix peas and celery. Season and place in serving bowl. Garnish with olives, pimentos and egg whites. Make a sauce of riced yolks, mayonnaise, lemon juice, sugar, and dill, and serve separately. If preferred, instead of using this sauce pour ½ cup French dressing over salad and sprinkle riced egg yolks on top.

Cabbage and Pineapple Salad

1 medium size Head
    Cabbage
1 cup Grated Pineapple
½ cup French Dressing

Shred cabbage very fine. Put in refrigerator to get crisp. Just before serving, mix with French dressing and pineapple, both of which have been previously chilled.

Cabbage, Pineapple and Carrot Salad

1 medium sized Cabbage
1 cup Grated Carrots
1 cup crushed Pineapple
½ cup French Dressing
½ cup Mayonnaise

Shred cabbage very fine. Grate or shred carrots. Mix all chilled ingredients just before serving.

Red Cabbage and Currant Salad

1 good sized Red Cabbage
½ glass Currant Jelly
½ cup Red Wine
Juice and Rind of 1 Lemon
1 tsp. Salt
Pinch of Pepper
2 Egg Whites
2 hard-boiled Eggs

Shred cabbage very fine (omit coarse stalks). Chill in refrigerator until crisp. Mix jelly, wine, lemon, salt and pepper together. Add stiffly beaten egg whites and fold in cabbage carefully. Garnish with hard-boiled eggs. or press yolks through a sieve or ricer and chop whites coarsely.

Cabbage, Carrot and Beet Salad

2 cups Grated Cabbage
2 cups Grated Carrots
2 cups Grated Raw Beets
1 large Head Lettuce
Russian Dressing

Grate or shred cabbage, carrots and beets. Arrange on lettuce leaves, alternating colors. Place bowl of Russian Dressing in middle. Serve very cold.

Marmalade and Cabbage Salad

1 medium Head Cabbage
1 cup Orange Marmalade
½ cup Mayonnaise
2 tbsp. Lemon Juice
1 tsp. Salt
Pinch of Pepper
Few grains Cayenne
½ cup heavy Cream

Shred cabbage very fine. Sprinkle with water and put in refrigerator to get crisp. In a large bowl, work marmalade until soft. Add lemon juice, salt, pepper, cayenne, mayonnaise and last, the whipped cream. With 2 forks, work in cabbage, making salad light and fluffy.

Fruit Marshmallow Mold

3 Eggs
½ cup Water
6 Marshmallows
Juice of 2 Lemons
1 tbsp. Vinegar
2 cups cubed Mixed
    Fruit (omit pineapple)
1 cup heavy Cream
pinch of Salt
1½ tbsp. Gelatine

Mix water, egg yolks, lemon juice vinegar and salt in double boiler, and stir until it thickens. Add marshmallows, and stir until they melt. Cool. Add gelatin, fruit, and fold in the stiffly whipped cream and beaten egg whites. Fill mold and let stand in cool place to set. Turn on platter and garnish with a border of watercress.

Salmon Salad with Vegetables

1½ cups cold Boiled Salmon
2 tomatoes
½ Cucumber
1 cup Boiled Peas
2 tsp. Lemon Juice
½ cup Mayonnaise
1 tsp. Sugar
1 tsp. Salt
Dash of Pepper

Flake salmon; cube tomatoes and cucumber (small cubes). Mix all together. Half fill small leaves of crisp lettuce. Place on platter and garnish with chopped parsley or dill.

Caviare and Beet Salad

1 cup each of Potatoes,
    Beets, Apples and
    Bananas
1 cup French Dressing
1 tbsp. Swedish Caviare
Few grains Cayenne
1 tbsp. Sugar

Cut up potatoes, beets, apples and bananas. Add Swedish caviar, cayenne and sugar to French dressing. Mix well and serve cold.

Kielerspraten and Egg Salad

4 Hard-boiled Eggs
½ cup Parsley
French Dressing

Skin and bone sprats. Chop egg yolks and whites separately. On a round dish arrange a star-like design using a row of whites, a row of yolks, one of sprats and one of chopped parsley. Place a small glass bowl of French dressing in center and servo cold.

Potato Salad

6-8 Medium Potatoes
½ cup Mayonnaise
½ cup Sliced Onions
½ cup White Vinegar
1 tbsp. Chopped Green
    Pepper
1 tsp. Sugar
1 tsp. Dry Mustard
Chopped Parsley
Salt — Pepper

Boil potatoes, peel and slice. While hot, fold in mixed ingredients. Let cool. When ready to serve, sprinkle with chopped parsley. Cold sliced potatoes may be used, but a decided improvement in flavor is obtained by using hot potatoes.

Turkey Salad in Cranberry Ring

1 qt. Cranberries
2 cups Sugar
Turkey or Chicken Salad

Boil cranberries in 2 cups water until soft. Press through strainer into saucepan. Do not let berries cool while straining. Add sugar and boil 5 minutes. Fill ring mold and let set over night. Turn out on platter and fill center with turkey or chicken salad.

Tomato and Cheese Ring

1 can Tomato Soup
2 pkgs. Cream Cheese
2 tbsp. Gelatine
½ cup Water
1 cup Mayonnaise
1½ cups chopped Celery
1 tbsp. Chopped Onions
2 Green Peppers, chopped

Heat tomato soup to boiling point and remove from fire. Add cheese and stir until well melted. Then add gelatin, previously dissolved in cold water. Salt to taste. When mixture is cooled, add vegetables and mayonnaise. Fill mold and let stand in refrigerator until set. Turn out on platter.

Beet Ring

6 Medium Beets
1 cup Cut Celery
2 tbsp. Chopped Green
    Pepper
½ cup Sugar
3 tbsp. Lemon Juice
½ cup White Vinegar
3 tbsp. Gelatine
Salt — Pepper

Wash and boil beets. Strain and save liquid. Skin beets and cut in small squares. Dissolve gelatin. Mix together all ingredients in 3 cups strained beet liquid and boil 5 minutes. Cool. Pour into ring mold and let set in refrigerator. Serve with cold meat or salad.

Avocado Salad

3 Avocadoes
French Dressing
Large Lettuce Leaves

Chill the pears. Skin by cutting only the skin in four places so as not to break the pear. Cut lengthwise in half and break away from stone. Fill hollows with French dressing and let stand 1 or 2 hours in refrigerator. Arrange each half on large lettuce leaf and serve.

Avocado and Grapefruit Salad

3 Avocadoes
1 seedless Grapefruit
1 head Romaine
Russian Dressing

Cut chilled pear in eight pieces lengthwise and peel. Wash and drain Romaine. Place leaves on a platter or a wide bowl, in star-like fashion. Place one piece of pear on each leaf and place sections of grapefruit between the leaves, near the edge. Place a small bowl filled with Russian dressing in middle of dish.

Fruit Salad

2 Bananas
1 cup Grapefruit
1 cup Oranges
1 cup Pineapple
½ cup Mixed Nuts

Cut up fruit. Crush nuts and mix with French or Russian Dressing.

Note: Any kind of fruit or variety of fruits makes a good salad if mixed with good dressing. If fruit is sour, add some sugar; if sweet, add lemon juice. Raw fruit should be cut up in small pieces or sliced thin, whereas cooked fruits look better whole, half or quartered.

Romaine and Banana Salad

1 Head Romaine
4 Bananas
Roquefort Dressing

Separate Romaine leaves. Wash and chill. With a fluted vegetable knife cut chilled bananas and place 4 or 5 pieces on each leaf of Romaine which has been arranged on a large platter in star-like fashion (root end in center). Pour a tablespoon of Roquefort dressing on bananas.

Banana and Strawberry Salad

3 Bananas
1 quart Strawberries
1 cup Heavy Cream
1 tbsp. Sugar
Few grains of Salt
Juice of one Lemon

Hull strawberies. Wash if necessary and dry well on towel. Cut bananas in ¼ inch slices crosswise. Whip cream with sugar and salt. Mix in lemon juice slowly. Pour over fruit and serve ice cold.

Pineapple Salad

1 large Pineapple
1 cup Mayonnaise
1 tbsp. Sugar
Pinch of Salt
½ cup Walnuts or Pecans

Trim the greens nicely and leave on fruit. Cut a slice off lengthwise. Carefully remove inside of fruit and slice. Mix with mayonnaise, sugar and salt. Refill pineapple shell. Garnish with halves of walnuts or pecans and serve very cold.

Pineapple Fruit Salad

1 large Pineapple
1 cup Apples
1 cup Bananas
1 cup mayonnaise
½ cup crushed walnuts

Prepare pineapple as above. Mix with other ingredients. Refill and serve cold.

Vegetable Mold

½ cup cooked Peas
½ cup each, cubed Carrots,
  Parsnips and Celery
2 tbsp. chopped Green Pepper
1 pkg. lemon-flavored Gelatin
1 tbsp. Vinegar
1 tbsp. Sugar

Cook peas with a pinch of salt, sugar and soda. Strain. Cook other vegetables together with vinegar, sugar and salt about 12 minutes in just enough water to cover. Do not overcook vegetables or they will look soggy. Prepare gelatin as directed on package; add green pepper and vegetables. Mold and chill until firm. Unmold and serve with cold cuts.
Note: Canned Macedoine or any and all kinds of left over vegetables may be used this way to good advantage.

Cottage Cheese and Carrot Mold

1 pkg. Orange-flavored
  Gelatin
½ lb. Cream Cheese
1 cup Grated Carrots
1 tbsp. Sugar
1 tbsp. A-1 Sauce
1 tsp. Paprika
1 tbsp. minced Parsley
Salt and Pepper

Dissolve orange-flavored gelatin in 1½ cups boiling water. Cool. Grate carrots, mix with cheese and add seasoning to taste. Gradually add cooled gelatin and pour mixture into a mold and chill until firm.

Cucumber Ring Mold

2 large Cucumbers
1 pkg. Lemon-flavored
  Gelatin
1 pkg. Lime-flavored
  Gelatin
1½ tbsp. Vinegar
Salt and Pepper
Tomatoes

Dissolve lemon and lime gelatin in 2 cups of hot water and cool. Grate cucumbers (skin, seeds and all); add water to make 2 cups; add vinegar, salt and pepper to taste. Stir in gelatin, mold and chill until firm. Unmold; fill center with watercress, place a border of sliced peeled tomatoes around and serve.

Fruit Salad Mold

2 pkgs. Lemon-flavored
  Gelatin
2 cups mixed cubed Fruit
1 Cup Mayonnaise
½ cup Cream
1 tsp. Salt
Sugar to taste.

Pour 2 cups of boiling water over lemon-flavored gelatin and cool. Mix fruit with mayonnaise, salt and a little sugar if needed. Add gelatin and fold in whipped cream. Mold and chill.

Shrimp in Aspic

1 lb. boiled and cleaned
    Shrimps
1 pkg. Lemon-flavored
    Gelatin
1 tbsp. plain Gelatin
½ tsp. Paprika
Dash of Tabasco
1 peeled Tomato
1 hard-boiled Egg
1 Green Pepper

Prepare lemon-flavored gelatin as directed on package; add plain gelatin which has been soaked in cold water. Cool. Pour small quantity in bottom of a mold; place shrimps, sliced eggs, green pepper and tomatoes in artistic design and then add remaining shrimps. Carefully fill mold with the rest of the gelatin and chill until firm.

Shrimp Mold

1 lb. boiled and cleaned
    Shrimps
1 pkg. Lime-flavored
    Gelatin
1 cup Mayonnaise
Few Grains Cayenne
Salt and Pepper

Slice or cube shrimps. Prepare gelatin as directed on package and when cool, mix all ingredients together. Mold and chill.

Alligator Pear Mold

4 large Pears
2 tbsp. Gelatin
1 tbsp. Lemon Juice
1 tbsp. Sugar
4 tbsp. Cream
½ cup Mayonnaise
Few Grains Cayenne
Salt and Pepper

Soak gelatin in ½ cup water; heat until melted. Peel pears and mash. Combine all ingredients, flavoring to taste. Mold and chill until firm. Unmold and garnish with a border of fancy cut pickled beets, tomatoes, lettuce or watercress.

Stuffed and other Vegetables

Stuffed Tomatoes with String Beans

Hot Stuffed Tomatoes

Stuffed Green Peppers No. 1

Stuffed Green Peppers No. 2

Hot Stuffed Green Peppers

Stuffed Mushrooms No. 1

Stuffed Mushrooms No. 2

Stuffed Eggplant No. 1

Stuffed Eggplant No. 2

Stuffed Celery Root

Stuffed Summer Squash

Stuffed Green Squash

Vegetable Filling

Stuffed Acorn Squash

Potato Cakes

Stuffed Alligator Pears

Stuffed Artichoke Bottoms

Jerusalem Artichokes

Celery-Cabbage with Tomatoes and Cottage Cheese

Stuffed Succini

Stuffed Cucumbers No. 1

Stuffed Cucumbers No. 2

Pickled Cucumbers (Swedish Style) "Pressgurka"

Spinach "Swedish Style"

Potato Surprise

Potato Souffle

Stuffed Tomatoes "Scandia"

Cauliflower Gratin

Stuffed Potatoes with Eggs

Stuffed Onions

Stuffed Tomatoes with String Beans

6 Medium Tomatoes
½ lb. Large String Beans
1 cup French Dressing
Few grains Cayenne
1 Hard-boiled Egg
1 head of Lettuce

Plunge tomatoes in boiling water few seconds and peel. Cut in half—remove pulp from center and drain. Cut string beans very thin crosswise; cook with pinch of soda 5 minutes; drain and cool. Marinate in French dressing to which few grains of cayenne have been added. Fill tomato halves. Decorate with strips of egg-white. Remove stalk and outside leaves from a crisp head of lettuce. Hold head of lettuce under cold running water until leaves separate, then carefully drain on towel. Place head on round dish or platter and bend leaves from head all around. Place filled tomatoes on the leaves and sprinkle with remainder of hard-boiled eggs.

Hot Stuffed Tomatoes

6 Medium Tomatoes (not too ripe)
½ cup Chopped Onions
½ cup Chopped Green Pepper
2 Hard-boiled Eggs, Chopped
1 tbsp. Chili Sauce
4 Whole Wheat Cracker Crumbs
1 tsp. Sugar
Salt to taste

Cut stem end of tomato, remove center and chop pulp. Saute with all other ingredients. Fill tomato shells and bake in moderate oven about 20 minutes.

Stuffed Green Peppers No. 1

4 large Green Peppers
4 Hard-boiled Eggs
1 small can Tomato Puree, or Ketchup
1 tbsp. Gelatin
Salt to taste

Remove stem end of pepper, and clean out the center. Peel hard-boiled egg and place inside of the pepper. Put toothpick through egg to hold in place. Fill surrounding space with tomato puree to which melted gelatin has been added. Place in refrigerator to set. Slice with sharp knife and serve on shredded lettuce.

Stuffed Green Peppers No. 2

4 medium Green Peppers
1 can Pimento
1 pkg. Cream Cheese
2 tbsp. Chopped Olives
1 tbsp. Gelatin
Salt — Pepper — Paprika
Shredded White Cabbage

Cut stem end of pepper and remove center. Line pepper inside with pimento and fill center with cream cheese to which chopped olives, melted gelatin, salt and pepper have been added. Chill in refrigerator. Slice carefully with sharp knife and serve on shredded white cabbage. Sprinkle with paprika.

Hot Stuffed Green Peppers

6 medium Green Peppers
1 cup Chopped Veal or
　　Chicken (left-over)
½ cup Chopped Onions
½ cup Boiled Rice
2 tbsp. Chili Sauce
1 cup Gravy or Stock
3 tbsp. Butter
3 Whole Wheat Crackers
Salt to taste

Cut stem end of pepper and remove center. Chop the part of pepper which you have cut off, with exception of stem and seed, and saute with onions. Add meat, chili sauce, rice, and stock. Salt to taste. Fill pepper. Sprinkle with buttered whole wheat cracker crumbs, and bake in moderate oven 20 minutes.

Stuffed Mushrooms No. 1

12 Mushrooms
2 Hard-boiled Eggs
1 Tomato
½ cup finely diced Chicken
½ cup Oil or Butter
Salt — Pepper

Select medium size white mushrooms with deep meaty caps. Break off stem and chop. Saute in butter for a few minutes. Add chopped tomatoes, chicken, and eggs. Add enough chicken gravy, stock or cream to moisten. Dip mushroom caps in olive oil or melted butter. Fill with mixture and bake about 10 minutes in hot oven or under broiler.

Stuffed Mushrooms No. 2

12 Mushrooms (large
　　meaty)
1 cup Tomatoes
½ cup Onions
1 tbsp. Green Pepper,
　　(Chopped)
½ cup Celery, Chopped
3 tbsp. Butter
1 tsp. Fuji Soy Sauce
4 Whole Wheat Crackers
Salt — Pepper

Prepare mushrooms same as in preceding recipe. Saute all other ingredients and season well. Fill mushroom caps. Sprinkle with buttered bread crumbs and bake 20 minutes.

Stuffed Eggplant No. 1

1 medium size Eggplant
1 cup Chopped Onions
1 cup Chopped Celery
1 cup Tomato Puree
½ cup Chopped Green
    Pepper
1 cup Boiled Rice
Few grains Cayenne
½ cup Butter
Salt to taste

Cut stem end of eggplant. Scoop out inside, leaving ½ inch shell around. Chop scooped out center and saute in butter. Add remaining ingredients. Cook 10 minutes. Season well, and fill shell. Cover with buttered bread crumbs and bake in moderate oven 30 minutes.

Stuffed Eggplant No. 2

1 large Eggplant
1 cup Minced Meat—
    Chicken or Veal "cooked"
1 cup Ground Ham
1 cup finely diced and
    cooked Carrots
6 Cracked Wheat Crackers
½ tsp. Curry
½ cup Chopped Parsley
½ tsp. Paprika
Salt — Pepper
Stock or Gravy

Cut stem end of eggplant, scoop out center (leaving ½ inch shell). Steam in stock or water 10 minutes. To this add all other ingredients and fill eggplant. Cover with buttered crumbs and bake 30 to 40 minutes in moderate oven.

Stuffed Celery Root

6 Celery Roots
½ lb. Raw Veal, ground
    fine
½ cup White Bread, soaked
    in cup milk
1 Egg
2 tbsp. Crumbs
1 tbsp. Chutney Sauce
½ tsp. Paprika
Salt — Pepper

Select medium size celery roots. Boil in salted water 20 minutes—not soft. Cool, peel, and scoop out center. Work meat with egg-yolk until very smooth. Mix inside of chopped celery root, meat, egg-yolk, bread with milk, chutney, paprika, salt and pepper. Last, fold in stiffly beaten eggwhite. Fill roots, and top with well buttered crumbs. Bake in slow oven 30 to 40 minutes. Note: Celery roots may also be stuffed same as Mushrooms No. 2.

Stuffed Summer Squash

6 Ind. Summer Squash
½ cup Chopped Green
    Pepper
1 cup Cooked Rice
½ cup Chopped Celery
½ cup Cream
Salt — Pepper

Boil squash 15 to 20 minutes. Cool and scoop out center. Chop and mix with green pepper, celery, cream, and salt and pepper to taste. Fill squash with mixture. Sprinkle with bread crumbs and bake 30 minutes.

Stuffed Green Squash

1 large Green Squash
1 lb. Beef (ground fine)
2 Eggs
1 cup Bread Crumbs
1 bottle Beer
1 tsp. Fuji Soy Sauce
½ cup Chopped Parsley
1 tsp. Salt
¼ tsp. Pepper
1 tsp. Sugar

Split a large green squash in two and bake in oven until it starts to soften. Remove from oven and scoop out center, leaving shell ¾ inch thick. Mix center of squash meat with bread crumbs and beer, and let stand at least 1 hour. Then add all other ingredients, folding in stiffly beaten eggwhites last. Fill one half shell with mixture and bake 1 hour. See following for other half:

Vegetable Filling

Vegetable Filling
Squash-meat
1 cup Small Peas
1 cup Small Cubed Carrots
1 cup Cut Celery
1 cup Butter
1 tbsp. Sugar
⅓ tsp. Mace
Salt — Pepper

For other half of squash shell, mix chopped squash with vegetables cooked only 15 minutes and strained. Add butter, sugar, mace, and salt and pepper to taste. Fill in shell and bake 30 minutes. Serve in shell, with any kind of roast meat.

Stuffed Acorn Squash

3 Acorn Squash
1 cup Ground Ham
2 tbsp. Green Pepper, Chopped
2 tbsp. Leeks or Scallions
½ cup Whole Wheat Cracker Crumbs
2 tbsp. Butter
1 tbsp. Fuji Soy Sauce
Salt and Pepper to taste

Bake whole squash in moderate oven 30 minutes. Saute green pepper and leeks in butter. Add ham, Soy sauce, and simmer for few minutes. Add crumbs and moisten with stock or water. Season well. Split squash scrape out seed, and fill cavity with mixture. Cover with crumbs and bake 20 minutes more. Pour over a tsp. of butter two or three times while baking.

Stuffed Alligator Pears

3 Alligator Pears
¼ lb. Pimento and Nut Cheese
1 tsp. Worcestershire Sauce
1 tbsp. Gelatin
1 tsp. Sugar
1 tbsp. Mayonnaise
Salt — Pepper

Split pears in two lengthwise. Peel. If cavity is small, scoop out some pear meat and mix with cheese. Add Worcestershire sauce, sugar, mayonnaise, and melted gelatin. Salt to taste. Fill cavity. Put the two halves together; wrap in wax paper, and keep in refrigeration for a few hours. Slice and serve on green chicory.

Stuffed Artichoke Bottoms

1 can Artichoke Bottoms
  (6 to 8 pieces)
½ cup Cubed Carrots
½ cup Cubed Celery
½ cup Small Peas
½ cup Mayonnaise
1 tbsp. Escoffier Sauce
1 tbsp. Gelatine
1 Chopped Truffle
1 Eggwhite
Salt — Pepper

Open can of artichokes and strain liquid into saucepan. Cut carrots and celery into very small cubes and boil in liquid. Cook peas separate. Mix melted gelatin with mayonnaise and escoffier sauce. Salt and pepper to taste. Add thoroughly chilled vegetables. Last, fold in stiffly beaten eggwhite. Fill artichoke bottoms with mixture and place same on bed of watercress.

Jerusalem Artichokes

1 lb. Jerusalem Artichokes
French Dressing
⅓ cup Chopped Walnuts or
  1 Truffle

Select small Jerusalem artichokes of even size. Boil slowly in salted water until soft. Cool, peel, and marinate in French dressing. Serve on red cabbage leaves. Sprinkle with crushed walnuts, or chopped truffles.

Celery-Cabbage with Tomatoes and Cottage Cheese

1 medium head Celery-
  Cabbage
3 Tomatoes
½ lb. Cottage Cheese
2 tbsp. Chopped Green
  Pepper
½ cup Thick Cream
Salt — Pepper

Cut celery-cabbage crosswise in 1 inch pieces. Peel and cut tomatoes in ¼ inch slices, and place on celery-cabbage. Top with spoon of cottage cheese previously mixed with cream, green pepper, and seasoning.

Stuffed Succini

2 Succini (2 lbs.)
½ lb. Liverpaste or Liverwurst
1 tsp. Escoffier Sauce
½ tsp. Salt
Pinch of Pepper
1 Egg
3 Whole Wheat Crackers
  (Crushed)
1 tbsp. Grated Cheese
2 tbsp. Bread Crumbs

In the East, succini is a comparatively new product. It is somewhat similar to a cucumber in appearance. Select small sizes about 2 inches in diameter. Cut in ½ inch pieces crosswise, leaving skin on. Scoop out part in middle of each slice. Chop and mix with other ingredients. Fill with mixture. Cover with mixed bread crumbs and grated cheese. Bake in hot oven 15 to 20 minutes.

Stuffed Cucumbers No. 1

2 large Cucumbers
1 Cream Cheese
1 Truffle, or 5 Ripe Olives
1 tbsp. Escoffier Sauce
2 tsp. Gelatin
Salt — Pepper

Split cucumber lengthwise. Scoop out seeds and soak cucumber in salted ice water for 1 hour. Mix cream cheese with chopped truffles or olives, escoffier sauce, and melted gelatin. Salt and pepper to taste. Fill cavities of cucumbers and tie together with strings. Cool and allow to set. Slice, and serve on romaine leaves.

Stuffed Cucumbers No. 2

2 large Cucumbers
2 cups Chopped Apples
2 hard-boiled Eggs, Chopped
1 cup Chopped, Mixed Pickles
¾ cup Russian Dressing
1 Eggwhite
1 tsp. Chopped Parsley

Split cucumber in two, lengthwise, and scrape out seeds. Place cucumbers in salted water 1 hour. Cut out part of inside, leaving ¼ inch shell. Chop cucumber and mix with other chopped ingredients. Add dressing and, last, stiffly beaten eggwhite. Salt and pepper to taste. Fill shells. Sprinkle with chopped parsley.

Pickled Cucumbers — Swedish Style (Pressgurka)

1 or 2 Cucumbers
1 cup White Vinegar
⅓ cup Sugar
2 Bay Leaf
6 Whole Allspice
Chopped Parsley
Pepper

Peel and slice cucumbers. Sprinkle with salt, and put in light press for 1 hour. Mix other ingredients and pour over cucumbers, first squeezing out juice. Serve with chopped parsley on top.

Spinach — Swedish Style

2 lbs. Spinach
1 cup Rich Cream Sauce
¼ tsp. Grated Nutmeg
1 tsp. Sugar
1 hard-boiled Egg
Salt — Pepper

Select young tender spinach. Wash thoroughly and steam wet leaves with pinch of soda 10 minutes. Mash through sieve. Mix with cream sauce, nutmeg, and sugar. Salt and pepper to taste. Decorate with egg — sliced quartered, or chopped.

Potato Surprise

2 cups Mashed Potatoes
1 Egg
2 tbsp. Butter
Roast Beef, Veal, Lamb or
    Chicken (left-overs)
Gravy (left-over)
1 tbsp. Chili Sauce, Chut-
    ney, or Escoffier
Salt — Pepper

Mix egg-yolk with potatoes, butter, salt and pepper to taste. Fold in stiffly beaten eggwhite. Press potatoes through a pastry tube in a small ring covering bottom of a buttered baking dish. Fill cavity with cubed meat mixed with gravy and sauce as desired. Top meat with potatoes and bake in hot oven until golden brown.

Potato Souffle

4 cups Mashed Potatoes
¼ cup Butter
2 Eggs
1 tbsp. Chopped Pimentos
1 tbsp. Chopped Parsley
1 tbsp. Blanched Almonds
    (finely chopped or
    grated)
Salt — Pepper

Mix all ingredients with 3 cups potatoes until very light. Fold in stiffly beaten eggwhites. Fill well-buttered baking dish ¾ full. Decorate top with remaining potatoes pressed through a pastry tube, and sprinkle with buttered crumbs. Brown in rather hot oven. Serve with any meat desired.

Stuffed Tomatoes (Scandia)

12 Small Tomatoes
½ cup Chopped Pickles
1 cup Chopped Apples
1 cup Chopped Beets
2 hard-boiled Eggs,
    Chopped
2 tbsp. Tarragon Vinegar
1 tbsp. Sugar
½ cup Mayonnaise
Salt — Pepper

Plunge tomatoes into hot water and peel. Cut stem end of tomato and remove center, turning upside down to drain. Mix juice and pulp with other ingredients. Season well and fill tomato shell. Serve on chicory salad leaves.

Cauliflower Gratin

1 Medium Size Cauliflower
1 Cream Cheese
1 tbsp. Lemon Juice
1 tsp. Sugar
¼ tsp. Nutmeg
½ cup Bread Crumbs, Soft
1 Egg
2 tbsp. Cream
Butter
Salt — Pepper

Boil cauliflower in water to which 2 tbsp. vinegar and 1 tbsp. salt have been added. When partly cooked, remove cauliflower and drain. Mix cream cheese with other ingredients. Spread over cauliflower. Sprinkle with bread crumbs and brown in oven. Baste with butter two or three times when starting to brown.

Potato Cakes

3 cups mashed Potatoes
2 Egg Yolks
½ tsp. Paprika
½ tsp. Celery Salt
Salt and Pepper
Bread Crumbs

Mix mashed potatoes with yolks and season to taste. Make small cakes, roll in bread crumbs and brown in frying pan.

Stuffed Potatoes with Eggs

6 large Potatoes
6 Eggs
Butter
Milk
Crumbs

Bake potatoes as usual. Cut a slice off lengthwise and scoop out potato leaving a border ½ inch thick inside of skin. Mash potatoes with butter, milk or cream, pepper and salt to taste. Break eggs carefully, using one yolk and only half of white in each potato. Sprinkle with a little salt and pepper and fill with mashed potatoes through a pastry tube. Sprinkle buttered crumbs on top, brown in oven and serve hot.

Note: The potatoes may be mixed with minced fish or meat if preferred.

Stuffed Onions

6 med. sized Spanish Onions
1 lb. Chopped Round Steak
1 cup grated raw Potatoes
2 tbsp. Chopped Onions
1 tsp. ground Allspice
1 or 2 Eggs
1 can Evaporated Milk
1 tbsp. Salt
¼ tsp. Pepper
Butter and crumbs

Peel and cut onions in half crosswise. Remove inside part of onion leaving 3 large outside layers for filling. Chop inside part and mix with all other ingredients. Let stand one hour or more to swell. Fill onion shells with mixture, sprinkle tops with buttered crumbs and bake in 350 degree oven about one-half hour. Serve with creamed vegetables.

Macaroni and Spaghetti Dishes

Macaroni Ring Mold	Fish and Macaroni Gratin
Spaghetti Swedish Style	Italian Spaghetti No. 1
Macaroni au Gratin	Italian Spaghetti No. 2
	Macaroni Salad

Spaghetti — Swedish Style

½ lb. Spaghetti
1 quart Milk or more
2 cups Meat
   Beef Lamb or Veal
   (cooked)
2 tbsp. Butter
1 tbsp. Onions
1 tbsp. Sugar
2 tsp. Salt
¼ tsp. Pepper
2 Eggs
2 tbsp. Parmesan Cheese

Add Spaghetti to boiling milk. Cook ten minutes with salt, sugar, and pepper. Chop onions, saute in butter; heat finely cut meat with onions. Beat eggs and mix all ingredients with spaghetti. Fill a buttered baking dish. Sprinkle cheese on top and brown in oven.

Macaroni Ring Mold

2 cups Cooked Macaroni
¼ lb. Liverwurst or
   Chicken Livers Sauted
2 Eggs
2 cups Cream Sauce
Butter
Salt — Pepper

Boil macaroni, and cut in small pieces. Mix with cream sauce to which liverwurst or chopped chicken livers have been added. Add egg yolks. Fold in stiffly beaten whites. Bake in buttered dish placed in pan of water for 30 minutes. Serve plain or with Piquant sauce.

Macaroni Au Gratin

½ lb. Macaroni
1 cup Grated Strong Cheese
3 cups Milk
3 tbsp. Butter
1 tbsp. Sugar
Salt and Pepper

Boil macaroni as directed on package. Make a thin cream sauce with butter, flour, milk, half cup cheese. Season with sugar, salt and pepper. Pour in a baking dish. Sprinkle with cheese and bake in oven until light brown.

Fish and Macaroni Gratin

½ lb. Macaroni
2 cups Cooked Fish
3 tbsp. Butter
1 tbsp. Flour
2 cups Milk
⅓ cup Chili Sauce
2 tbsp. White Bread
    Crumbs

Boil macaroni in water with one teaspoon salt. Drain. Make a sauce of butter, flour, milk (or half milk and half fish bouillon) and cook five minutes. Add Chili sauce, season to taste. Add fish and macaroni and mix carefully. Pour in buttered baking dish. Sprinkle with bread crumbs and brown slightly in oven.

Italian Spaghetti No. 1

½ lb. Spaghetti
1 lb. Top Round
1 cup Bouillon
1 cup Chopped Onions
½ cup Ketchup
Salt, Pepper, Cayenne

Boil spaghetti in salted water. Drain. Cut beef in tiny strips and brown with onions twenty minutes. Add ketchup, bouillon, salt, pepper and a few grains Cayenne. Add spaghetti, heat well and serve hot.

Italian Spaghetti No. 2

1 lb. Spaghetti
½ lb. Bacon
2 cups Onions
1 Green Pepper
2 cups Tomatoes
1 can Italian Tomato
    Paste
½ cup Parsley
Parmesan Cheese

Cut bacon in fine strips or cubes. Fry three minutes, add chopped onions. Fry three minutes more and add chopped green pepper, tomatoes, paste and parsley, let simmer 10 to 15 minutes. Cook spaghetti in salted water ten minutes. Drain well and place on deep dish or platter. Pour sauce over and serve hot with grated cheese on the side.

Macaroni Salad

Large Macaroni
Left-over Ox Tongue, Ham
    or Smoked Beef
French Dressing
Chili Sauce

Boil large macaroni; drain and cool. Cut crossways in tiny rings. Cut meat in narrow strips, one inch long. Add Chili Sauce to French dressing. Mix all together and serve cold. If desired, omit French dressing and serve dish hot.

Canape and Sandwiches

for Cocktails, Teas and Suppers

In a well kept household one should never need worry if unexpected guests drop in of an afternoon or evening for a cocktail and a snack.

Use left-overs from meals. Cut, chop or grind fish, meat, vegetables, etc., and mix with relishes, mayonnaise, gravy sauces, pickles, tartare sauce, or whatever there is, to make a tasty spread.

Any kind of good bread, including Swedish Health Bread, Boston Brown Bread, Round and Finger Rolls, Baking Powder Biscuits, etc., may be used. Cut into any shape desired. If bread is stale, toast - - - otherwise, use fresh bread. Spread with soft butter or mayonnaise, and to make sandwiches attractive, garnish with sliced black or stuffed olives, green pepper, string beans, cooked peas, beets, pimento, pickles, radishes, dill, parsley, chopped hard-boiled eggs, etc.

With a little training and ingenuity, one can produce a variety of palatable snacks which will be well worth the trouble.

For Rolled Sandwiches, use the lightest kind of bread. Remove crust, and cut in very thin slices lengthwise. Spread with soft butter mixed with any colorful fillings—such as chopped pimento, green pepper, pistachio nuts, ground tongue, etc. Make one or more fillings. Roll bread—tighten wax paper around, and keep in refrigerator until needed. Slice in thin slices crosswise, and serve.

To make a Sandwich Surprise, cut off all crusts from a loaf of white bread (not too fresh). Slice five even pieces lengthwise. Spread one slice with butter and ground ham, one with pimento cheese, one with crushed pistachio nuts mixed with mayonnaise, and one with chopped eggs mixed with cream or mayonnaise. Stack, and cover entirely with cream cheese mixed with mayonnaise. Serve on a large platter garnished with olives, stuffed celery, radishes. green peppers, mixed pickles, etc. Cut at table when serving.

Slice white chicken or turkey. Season, and top with smaller slice of cranberry jelly; or, cut a round slice of cranberry jelly and place on a larger piece of white bread with chicken or turkey on top.

Place a thin slice of smoked salmon on buttered bread. Place a slice of hard-boiled egg on top of the salmon, and 2 thin strips of green pepper on the egg.

Peel and stone 1 alligator pear. Mash. Season with salt, pepper, sugar, lemon juice, and a few grains of cayenne or tabasco. Spread on potato chips, crackers, or bread.

Place a slice of tomato on bread and sprinkle with salt and pepper. Top with a slice of white chicken, and garnish with cooked string beans cut lengthwise, or with strips of green pepper. (Any left over roast may be used in place of chicken.)

Kielerspraten Canape No. 1

Skin and bone 6 sprats. Slice 6 squares of Pumpernickel and cut off crust. Spread with mayonnaise. Chop the white and yolk of a hard-boiled egg separately. Dip edges of bread, half of canapés in white and half in yolks. Put two filets on each canapé and place alternately on platter.

Kielerspraten Canape No. 2

Skin and bone sprats. Cut bread same size as sprat. Spread bread with butter or mayonnaise and dip edges in finely chopped parsley. Place a filet on each and serve.

Kielerspraten Canape No. 3

Skin and bone sprats, mash and add a few grains cayenne. Mix in enough mayonnaise to spread. Cut thin slices of Boston Brown Bread. Spread on mixture and garnish with slices of stuffed olives.

Bird's Nest Canape

Separate yolks and whites of six raw pullet eggs. Cut 2 onions crosswise and save 6 rings large enough to hold egg yolk. Cut Boston Brown Bread one-half inch larger. Skin, bone and mash 6 anchovies. Add mayonnaise (about 1 tablespoonful) and stiffly beaten egg whites. Through a pastry tube put a border of mixture on onion ring and fill edge with finely chopped onions.

Chop left-over fish and mix with chili sauce cr tomatoes, chopped cucumber, and any cooked vegetable. Season and mix well.

Mix finely diced cold lamb with chcw chow or dill pickles and some cooked vegetables, together with lamb gravy. Season.

Mix fresh or canned salmon with mayonnaise. Garnish with whole capers or pickles.

Hot Chicken and Mushroom Canapé

4 soft English Muffins
2 cups minced Chicken
1 lb. Mushrooms
1/3 cup Butter
2 tbsp. Flour
1 cup Chicken Soup
1 cup rich Milk
2 tbsp. minced Chutney
1 tsp. Celery Salt
Salt and Pepper

Select white meaty mushrooms of any size. Break off stems and boil in a little water or stock and use this broth in cream sauce. Break caps in pieces and saute in butter 3 or 4 minutes. Sprinkle flour on top, add broth, chicken soup, milk and seasoning. Then add chicken and bring to a boil. Split muffins, toast on both sides, butter them and place a half on each plate. Heap on chicken mixture, garnish and serve hot.

Lobster Patties

8 open Pastry Shells
2 cups cubed boiled Lobster
4 tbsp. Butter
2 tbsp. Flour
1½ cups light Cream
2 Egg Yolks
Few grains Cayenne
1/3 cup Sherry
Salt and Pepper

Heat lobster and sherry in double boiler. Melt butter, add flour, cream, cayenne, salt and pepper to taste, and let boil a few minutes. Pour over lobster. Add egg yolks mixed with a little cream. Heat, but do not boil. Fill warm shells, garnish and serve hot.

Lobster Canapé

8 slices White Toast
8 large Mushrooms
½ lb. Mushrooms (any size)
2 cups cubed boiled Lobster
1 tbsp. Flour
½ cup Butter
1 cup rich Milk
½ tsp. Paprika
½ cup Sherry
3 egg Yolks
Salt and Pepper

Cut away the wooden part of large mushroom stems. Brush with butter, sprinkle with salt, pepper and paprika. Peel, break and saute other mushrooms in remaining butter for a few minutes. Sprinkle flour on top, add seasoning, milk, and let boil 3 minutes. Add sherry and lobster, and last, the egg yolks mixed with 2 tbsp. milk. Heat but do not boil. Fill mushroom caps, around stems, bake in moderate oven fifteen to twenty minutes, place on toast, garnish and serve hot.

Chicken and Cream Cheese Canapé

8 slices White Bread
    (Diamond shaped)
½ lb. Cream Cheese
2 cups minced Chicken
½ cup Mayonnaise
½ tsp. Celery Salt
1 tbsp. grated Horseradish
3 tbsp. Cream
Few grains Cayenne
Salt and Pepper
Green Pepper
Pimento

Toast bread on one side and butter the other. Mix chicken with mayonnaise, celery salt, horseradish and seasoning to taste. Place a mound of mixture in diamond shape on bread. Mix cheese with cream, cayenne, salt and pepper and with a pastry tube make an attractive border on edge of bread. Garnish chicken with narrow strips of green pepper and pimento or tomatoes and serve cold.

Hot Fish Canapé

8 open individual
    Pastry Shells
4 cups boiled Fish
4 tbsp. Butter
3 tbsp. Flour
1 cup Cream
1 cup Fish Broth or Milk
1 tbsp. minced Pimento
1 tbsp. minced Parsley
Dash Tabasco
Salt and Pepper

Melt butter. Add flour, fish broth or milk, cream and seasoning. Boil for a few minutes. Fold in flaked fish (not minced), and serve in warm shells. Surround with a border of hot cubed beets if desired.

Hot Individual Luncheon Canapés

1 cup Rice
8 slices White Bread
3 cups minced cooked Veal
3 tbsp. Butter
2 tbsp. Flour
1 cup Cream or Rich Milk
1 cup Veal Broth or Gravy
1 tsp. Curry
1 tbsp. Sugar
1 tbsp. minced parsley
Salt and Pepper

Wash rice and put it in a double boiler. Pour boiling water over rice until a level of one inch above rice is reached. Add 1 tbsp. salt, cover and steam until rice is cooked but not soggy. In another pan, melt butter, add flour, cream, gravy or broth, curry dissolved in 1 tbsp. water, sugar, salt and pepper to taste. When well blended, add the veal. Toast bread and shape into rounds. Cut a one-inch round from center of each large round. Roll edges of small rounds in butter and then in parsley, and use as garnishing.
Place large toast on individual plates. With a small ice cream scoop or demi tasse cup, place a mound of rice on toast, surround with creamed meat. Place small toast on top of rice like a hat and serve.

Stuffed Shrimp Canapé

12 boiled and cleaned
    Shrimps
12 rounds of Bread
3 hard boiled Eggs
1 tbsp. Anchovy or
    Sardine Paste
2 tbsp. Mayonnaise
Salt and Pepper if needed.

Split shrimps and place two halves on each round of bread. Cut eggs with slicer, mash yolks with fish paste, mayonnaise and seasoning. With pastry tube make a rose between the halves of shrimp and use the ring of egg white as a border.

Sardellen Canapé

8 square slices Toast
2 cans Sardellen
3 hard boiled Eggs
Mayonnaise
Parsley
Lettuce

Remove crusts from toast and spread squares with mayonnaise. Squeeze whole eggs through potato ricer evenly over bread. Cut sardellen in half lengthwise and place them in squares on top of eggs. Place a speck of parsley in each square. Tear crisp lettuce in small pieces and arrange on a salad plate. With a spatula place canapes on top. Serve very cold.

Sardine Canapé

8 square slices Bread
1 glass Pimento Cheese
2 cans Sardines (large)
Stuffed olives
1 head Romaine Salad

Toast bread on one side and remove crusts. Spread with pimento cheese. Split sardines in half and place 3 or 4 halves on each slice of bread, using sliced olives as a border. Place a crisp leaf of Romaine at each corner of bread and serve cold.

Anchovy Canapé

8 slices Boston Brown Bread
1 large can skinless and
    boneless Anchovies
4 hard boiled Eggs
Cooked Beets
Watercress
Butter

With a fluted knife, cut medium sized beets and marinate in French Dressing for an hour or more. Drain and dry beets and place on buttered bread. Place sliced egg around beets in border form. Cut anchovies in half lengthwise and place on edge of yolks. Serve cold with crisp watercress.

Shrimp Canapé

8 slices Boston Brown Bread
3 doz. medium sized cooked
    Shrimps
Mayonnaise
Black Olives
Garnishing.

Peel shrimps and remove dark sand vein. Split in half lengthwise and place in a circle on bread which has been spread with mayonnaise. Garnish with strips of black olives and place one whole olive in center of canape.

Crawfish Canapé

24 medium sized Crawfish
8 thin slices Pumpernickel
Butter
Mayonnaise
Dill
½ cup finely chopped Celery
Note: Crabmeat may be used in the same manner, leaving the meat from the claws whole and using the small pieces mixed with celery and mayonnaise for the sides.

Wash crawfish and be sure they are alive when ready to cook. Pour 3 quarts boiling water with ½ cup salt and few sprays of dill over fish and boil 8 to 12 minutes according to size. Let cool in water. Remove the tail carefully and from that remove the dark sand vein. Remove the meat from the claw and stomach, add the roe (if any) and mix with celery and enough mayonnaise to hold mixture together. Place 3 or more fish tails on each buttered slice of pumpernickel and garnish sides with the mixture. Place a fresh green spray of dill on top and serve.

Cottage Cheese Canapé

8 rounds Cracked Wheat Bread
1 lb. Cottage Cheese
3 or 4 large Tomatoes
½ cup Cream
Butter
Dill Pickles
Paprika, Salt and Pepper

Butter rounds of bread and place a slice of peeled tomato on top of each. Sprinkle with salt, pepper and a little sugar. Work cheese with cream, paprika, salt and pepper to taste and with an ice cream scoop, place a ball of cheese on top of tomato. Slice pickles and make a border around the edge of bread.

Ham on Tongue Canapé

4 large Soda Biscuits
1 cup minced Ham or Tongue
½ cup mayonnaise
2 tbsp. Chopped Dill Pickles
2 cups evenly sliced Carrots
1 tbsp. Lemon Juice
1 Orange
2 tbsp. Sugar
1 tsp. Salt
3 tbsp. Butter
4 Stuffed Olives

Boil carrots in 2 cups water with lemon juice, grated rind and juice of orange, sugar, salt and butter, until water has evaporated. Carrots should then be cooked but will not be soft. Mix minced meat with mayonnaise and chopped pickles and spread on split biscuits. Place a border of carrots around edge and a half olive in center.

Sandwich Spreads

Any of the following spreads may be used for open sandwiches:

Left-over scrambled eggs highly seasoned. Sprinkle with chopped parsley and place a slice of broiled bacon on top.

Chop hard-boiled eggs very fine. Mix with anchovy paste and enough mayonnaise to spread easily.

Chop hard-boiled eggs very fine. Mix with mayonnaise, and spread on bread. Place ½ anchovy on top. Sardellen or sardines may also be used in the same manner (boned and skinned).

Mince roast beef and mix with finely chopped cold potato, grated horseradish and salad dressing. Season, and mix well.

Mix equal parts of chopped chicken, nuts and celery and good chicken gravy to spread. Season well.

Saute chicken livers. Cool, chop, and mix with A-1 Sauce.

Saute chicken livers in butter. Chop and mix with finely chopped chicken. Add cream sauce. Season well and serve hot.

Saute chicken livers in chicken fat or butter, but do not brown. Mash, and mix with an equal amount of finely chopped olives or sweet pickles, and add mayonnaise to spread. Season well.

Saute and grind calves' liver. Melt a small amount of butter; add liver and a few bread crumbs, chili sauce or tomato catsup, and mix well. Season and serve cold, or brown under broiler and serve hot.

Decorate liverpaste with strips of beets, green olives, or red pepper—or, make a paste of good liverwurst with any tasty pickles, olives or chow chow. Add a little whipped or plain cream.

Fry calves' liver. Put through food chopper twice and add mayonnaise. Season well. Place a piece of crisp bacon on top after spreading on bread, and heat under broiler.

Fry and chop chicken or calf livers. Strain liquid from one can of corn. Mix chopped liver with corn and season well.

Slice cold meat balls and top with slices of dill pickles.

Spread a thin layer of caviar (unsalted is best) on a slice of bread (round shape). Garnish with hard-boiled eggs, the yolks and whites of which have been chopped separately.

Mixed left-over mashed potatoes with finely cut pickled herring. Add chopped chives or parsley.

Place a thin layer of bottled horseradish (squeezed dry) on bread. Top with a thin slice of rare roast beef.

Select tiny leaves of lettuce from the heart. Fill with finely cut apples and celery, mixed with mayonnaise, and sprinkle with chopped walnuts.

Marinate thin slices of sweet potatoes in French dressing. Place on bread, then add a smaller slice of pickled beet and hard-boiled egg. Top with a fancy cut radish.

Place a round slice of cooked carrot on bread, then a slice of pickled beet, followed with a slice of pickled cucumber. Top with half ripe or green olives, making the sandwich pyramid shaped.

Soften 1 package of cream cheese with milk, and beat until creamy and light. Add a pinch of salt and 2 tbsp. finely chopped pickled or candied ginger.

On a layer of chopped mixed pickles or chow chow, place a slice of liverwurst. Garnish with strips of beets.

Mix cranberry jelly with chopped pistachio and almonds.

Mix Roquefort and cream cheese with chopped celery and olives. Soften with cream or mayonnaise.

To cream cheese, add orange pulp removed from skins. Season with salt and a few grains of cayenne.

To 1 package of Philadelphia cream cheese add ½ tsp. of grated onions; 3 tbsp. finely chopped nutmeat (any kind); 1 tbsp. finely chopped green pepper; and a pinch of salt. Soften to desired consistency and spread.

To 1 package of Philadelphia cream cheese, add enough milk to spread. Add 2 tbsp. chopped candied cherries and a pinch of salt.

To 1 package cream cheese, add 1 tbsp. finely sliced Maraschino cherries; 1 tbsp. finely chopped or grated almonds, and a pinch of salt. Soften with mayonnaise, cream or milk, to spread easily, or garnish with sliced cherry rings.

Pound to a paste equal parts of cheese and walnuts. Add 1 tbsp. Worcestershire sauce or A-1 sauce, a pinch of salt, and enough cream to moisten.

Melt equal parts of Roquefort and butter to a creamy consistency. Add a pinch of salt; few grains of cayenne; 1 tsp. Worcestershire sauce, and 1 tbsp. of brandy. Beat until foamy.

Add chopped crisp bacon and chopped gherkins to mixed Roquefort and cream cheese which has been thinned with mayonnaise or cream to spread easily.

Spread cream cheese on crackers with wine or cranberry jelly in center.

Work cottage cheese with wooden spoon or fork until it is a smooth paste. Season. Add a little thick cream or mayonnaise. Chili sauce may also be used. Good on whole wheat crackers.

Grind or grate dried pieces of cheese and mix with thick cream sauce. Spread on bread or crackers. Toast and serve hot.

Mix 1 cup of grated mixed cheese with ½ cup stale white bread crumbs, 1 tsp. Worcestershire, ½ tsp. prepared mustard, salt and paprika. Add 2 egg-yolks and 1 tbsp. butter. Spread on bread or crackers and bake in hot oven or brown under broiler.

Garnishing

Some of the dishes which have been photographed may seem a bit elaborate and appear to entail a great deal of work, but they are as easily prepared in a private home as in the cuisines of the finest restaurants.

A little extra time spent in garnishing can make the simplest platters look most appetizing and artistic. Green borders are so easily arranged by using any of the following which are obtainable all the year round, i.e. parsley, lettuce, watercress, chicory, escarole, cabbage, celery tops, etc. Furthermore, such vegetables as radishes, beets, carrots, parsnips, celery, turnips, etc., cut in fancy shapes like roses, fans, combs, and leaves, and then kept in ice water until they spread to pretty shapes, make excellent and colorful decorations. Gelatin in small molds or cut in various figures, red and green peppers, pimentoes, tomatoes, eggs, black, green and stuffed olives — all are used with great effect.

Note: Desserts like puddings, whips, etc., may be made richer by adding whipped cream and lighter with additional beaten eggwhites.

Cocktails, Etc.

The success of a party or dinner many times depends on the selection of drinks that are served with the food.

Most people know how to drink and enjoy a cocktail but few know how to make them. The following recipes will give the host or hostess full instructions as to the mixing of all well-known cocktails, cobblers, egg noggs, flips, sours, toddies, etc.

The host or hostess may follow with assurance the directions given for the creation and the serving of drinks on all occasions as most of the recipes are reprinted from Mr. Knut Sundin's book "Two Hundred Selected Drinks" which is now out of print. Mr. Sundin has been for many years the chief bartender on the flagships of the Swedish American Line.

Alexander Cocktail.

Fill the shaker half full of broken ice and add:
- 2/3 of Creme of Cocoa
- 1/3 of Gin
- Fresh cream

Shake well and strain into a cocktail glass.

Aquarium Cocktail.

Fill a shaker half full with broken ice and add:
- 2/3 Bacardi Rum
- 1/3 Cointreau
- The juice of half a lime

Shake well and strain into a cocktail glass.

Bacardi Cocktail.

Fill the shaker half full of broken ice and add:
2/3 of Bacardi rum, the juice of half a lime, sugar syrup according to taste. Shake well and strain into a cocktail glass.

Bachelors Club Cocktail.

Fill the shaker half full of broken ice and add:
- 1/3 of brown cream of Cocoa
- 1/3 of Brandy
- 1/3 of fresh cream

Shake well and strain into a cocktail glass.

Brandy Cocktail.

Fill the bar glass half full of broken ice and add:

One or two dashes of Angostura bitters
3 dashes of Curacao
One glass of Brandy

Stir upp well, strain into a cocktail glass.

Bronx Cocktail.

Fill the shaker half full of broken ice and add:

The juice of a quarter of an orange
1/2 of Dry Gin
1/4 of Dry Vermouth
1/4 of Italian Vermouth

Shake well and strain into a cocktail glass.

Champagne Cocktail.

In a champagne glass put a lump of sugar, soak
it with Angostura Bitters, squeeze the essence of
two or three lemon peels in the glass, add a lump
of ice and fill the glass with iced Champagne,
stir up slightly with the mixing spoon, squeeze and
drop another piece of lemon peel in the glass.

Clover Club Cocktail.

Fill the shaker half full of broken ice and add:

The white of a fresh egg
The juice of a small fresh lime or of a lemon
One teaspoon of Grenadine syrup
2/3 of Dry Gin
1/3 of Dry Vermouth

Shake well and strain into a wine glass.

Cuban Manhattan Cocktail.

Fill the shaker half full of broken ice and add:

Half a cocktail glass of Bacardi Rum
Half a cocktail glass of Italian Vermouth
A few drops of Angostura bitters

Shake well and strain into a cocktail glass.

Daiquiri Cocktail.

Fill the shaker half full of broken ice and add:

2/3 of Bacardi
The juice of a fresh lime
Sweeten with Grenadine

Shake well and strain into a cocktail glass.

Doctor's Cocktail.

Fill the shaker half full of broken ice and add:

2/3 of a glass of Swedish Punsch
1 dash of Angostura bitters
1/3 of lemon juice

Shake well and strain into a cocktail glass.

Dubonnet Cocktail.

Fill a bar glass half full of broken ice and add:

2/3 of Dubonnet
1/3 of Gin

Stir up and strain into a cocktail glass.
Squeeze lemon peel on top.

Eternal Sunshine.

Fill the shaker half full of broken ice and add:

The juice of half a lemon
Half a glass of Dry Gin
Half a glass of Swedish Punsch
2 dashes of Grenadine syrup

Shake well, strain into a cocktail glass and add a cherry.

Greta Garbo Cocktail.

Fill the shaker half full of broken ice and add:

The juice of half a lime
3 dashes of Grenadine
1 dash of Absinthe
1/3 of Cointreau
2/3 of Bacardi Rum

Shake well and strain into a cocktail glass.

Jack Rose Cocktail.

Fill the shaker half full of broken ice and add:

The juice of a fresh lime or lemon
2/3 glass of Apple Jack Brandy
A teaspoonful of grenadine syrup

Shake well and strain into a cocktail glass.

Manhattan Cocktail.

Fill a bar glass half full of broken ice and add:

1 or 2 dashes of Angostura bitters
2/3 of Rye Whisky
1/3 of Italian Vermouth

Stir well, strain into a cocktail glass and add a cherry.

Marconi Cocktail.

Fill the bar glass half full of broken ice and add:

2 dashes of Angostura bitters
2/3 of Dry Gin
1/3 of Italian Vermouth

Stir up and strain into a cocktail glass, add a cherry.

Martini Cocktail (Dry).

Fill the bar glass half full of broken ice and add:

1 dash of Orange bitters
2/3 of Dry Gin
1/3 of Dry Vermouth

Stir up and strain into a cocktail glass, squeeze lemon peel on top add an olive.

Martini Cocktail (Sweet).

Fill the bar glass half full of broken ice and add:

1 dash of Orange bitters
2/3 of Dry Gin
1/3 of Italian Vermouth

Stir up and strain into a cocktail glass, add a cherry.

Millionaire Cocktail.

Fill the shaker half full of broken ice and add:

The white of a fresh egg
2   dashes of Curacao
1/3 of Grenadine syrup
2/3 of Rye Whisky

Shake well and strain into a small wine glass.
A dash of Absinthe may be added if desired.

Milk Of The Wild Cow Cocktail.

Fill the shaker half full of broken ice and add:

2/3 of Dry Gin
1/3 of Grenadine
1   teaspoonful of fresh cream

Shake well and strain into a cocktail glass.

Masolle Cocktail.

Fill a shaker half full of broken ice and add:

One glass of Brandy
Half a glass of Absinthe
Three dashes of Cointreau liqueur
The juice of 1/4 of a lemon

Shake well and strain into a cocktail glass.

Olle Cocktail.

Recipe by Olle, the well known bartender of te Vikings in Paris.

Put a large lump of ice in a tumbler and add:

Half a cocktail glass of Gin
Half a cocktail glass of Cointreau
Fill the balance with Champagne

Orange Blossom Cocktail.

Half a cocktail glass of dry Gin and half a glass of fresh orange juice, iced and well shaken with two dashes of orange bitters. Two or three dashes of Grenadine syrup, if desired sweet.

Pick-me-up Cocktail.

Fill the shaker half full of broken ice and add:

The juice of half a lemon
3/6 of Brandy
2/6 of Jamaica Rum
1/6 of Grenadine syrup
5 dashes of Maraschino

Shake well and strain into a cocktail glass.

Rose Cocktail.

Fill a shaker half full of broken ice and add:

1 dash of lemon juice
1/4 Cherry Brandy
1/4 Dry Vermouth
1/2 Dry Gin

Shake well and strain into a cocktail glass.
Frost edge of cocktail glass with sugar.

Sherry Cocktail.

Fill the bar glass half full of broken ice and add:

4 dashes of Orange bitters
One glass of Dry Sherry Wine

Stir well and strain into a cocktail glass.

Cherry Brandy Cocktail.

Fill the bar glass half full of broken ice and add:

1/5 of Cherry Brandy
1/5 of Italian Vermouth
2/5 of Dry Vermouth
1/5 of Dry Gin

Stir up and strain into a cocktail glass, add a cherry.

Side Car Cocktail.

Fill the shaker half full of broken ice and add:

3 dashes of lemon juice
Half a glass of Cointreau
Half a glass of Brandy

Shake well and strain into a cocktail glass.

Silver Cocktail.

Fill the bar glass half full of broken ice and add:

3 dashes of Orange bitters
1 dash of sugar syrup
3 dashes of Maraschino
Half a glass of Dry Vermouth
Half a glass of Dry Gin

Stir up and strain into a cocktail glass.

Stinger Cocktail.

Fill the shaker half full of broken ice and add:

2/3 of Brandy
1/3 of Green Creme de Menthe

A dash of Absinthe gives a good taste to this drink.

Shake well and strain into a cocktail glass.

Virginia Cocktail.

Fill the shaker half full of broken ice and add:

1 glass of Gin
1 teaspoonful of sugar of syrup

Shake well and strain into a cocktail glass, add a cherry.

Cobblers.

The cobblers are long drinks, they are very refreshing during hot weather, They can be made with almost any kind of wines and also with whisky, gin, brandy.

Brandy Cobbler.

Fill a tumbler 2/3 full of broken ice and add:

The juice of half a lemon
Sugar according to taste
2 glasses of Rhine wine
One and a half glass of Brandy

Fill upp with cold soda water, decorate the top with fruit in season and serve with straws and a spoon.

Champagne Cobbler.

Fill a tumbler 2/3 of broken ice and add:

The juice of an orange
A teaspoon full of sugar
Half a glass of raspberry syrup
One glass of Brandy

Fill upp with Champagne, decorate with fruit in season and serve with straws.

Claret Cobbler.

Fill a tumbler 2/3 full of broken ice and add:

The juice of half a lemon
Sugar according to taste
One and a half glass of Claret
Half a glass of Brandy

Fill upp with cold soda water and stir up, decorate the top neatly with slices of fruit in season, serve with straws and a spoon.

Cosmopolitan Cobbler.

Fill a tumbler 2/3 full of broken ice and add:

The juice of half a lemon
Sugar according to taste
One glass of Brandy
One glass of Portwine

Fill up with cold soda water, decorate with the peel of a cucumber and slices of fruit in season, serve with straws and a spoon.

Sherry Cobbler.

Fill a tumbler half full of broken ice and add:

The juice of half a lemon
Sugar according to taste
2 glass of Sherry wine

Fill up with cold soda water and stir up, decorate with fruit slices serve with straws and a spoon.

Whisky Cobbler.

Fill a tumbler 3/4 full of broken ice and add:

The juice of half a lemon
Sugar according to taste
2 glasses of Mosel wine
Half a glass of Whisky

Fill up with soda water, decorate the top with fruit in season, serve with straws and a spoon.

Tip Top Cobbler.

Fill a tumbler 2/3 full of broken ice and add:

The juice of half a lemon
Sugar according to taste
Half a glass of Brandy
Half a glass of Brown Curacao

Fill up with Champagne, decorate the top with slices of fruit in season, serve with straws and a spoon.

Egg Noggs.

Breakfast Egg Nogg.

The ingredients are:

1 fresh egg
Half a cocktail glass of Orange Curacao
One cocktail glass of Brandy
Balance with rich milk

Ice well, shake and strain into a tumbler. Grate cinnamon on top.

Egg Nogg.

Fill the shaker half full of broken ice and add:

1 fresh egg
1 teaspoonful of sugar syrup
2/3 of Brandy
1/3 of Rum
Balance with rich milk

Shake well and strain into a tumbler. Add grated nutmeg on top.

Eye Opener.

A good eye opener is made as following:

1 fresh egg
1/3 of Old good Brandy
1/3 of Absinthe
1/3 of Green Creme de Menthe

Ice well and shake, strain into a wine glass. If this drink does not open the eyes, add a small pinch of red pepper on the top. This will do it properly, and give you a glad eye at the same time.

Night Cap.

For a good night cap the ingredients are:

The yolk of a fresh egg
1/3 of Anisette
1/3 of Curacao
1/3 of Brandy

Ice well and shake, strain into a small wine glass.

Plain Egg Nogg.

Fill the shaker half full of broken ice and add:

1 fresh egg
1 teaspoonful of sugar syrup
One wine glass of Brandy, Whisky, Gin or
    Rum, according to taste
Fill the balance with rich milk

Shake well and strain into a tumbler. Add grated nutmeg on top.

Fizzes.

Brandy Fizz.

Fill the shaker half full of broken ice and add:

The juice of half a lemon
Sugar according to taste
1 glass of Brandy

Shake well, strain into a tumbler and fill up with cold soda water.

Gin Fizz.

Fill the shaker half full of broken ice and add:

A teaspoonful of sugar syrup
The juice of one lemon
1 glass of Dry Gin

Shake well, strain into a tumbler and fill up with cold soda water. Serve and drink immediately.

Gin Rickey Fizz.

Put a few lumps of ice in a tumbler, cut a good size lime in half, drop it into the glass, add one glass of Dry Gin, fill up with cold soda water and serve with a spoon.

Golden Fizz.

A golden fizz is a gin fizz to which the yolk of an egg has been added.

Manhattan Fizz.

Fill the shaker half full of broken ice and add:

The juice of half a lemon
Sugar according to taste
1 glass of Italian Vermouth
1 glass of Rye Whisky

Shake well, strain into a tumbler and fill up with cold soda water.

Martini Fizz.

Fill the shaker half full of broken ice and add:

The juice of half a lemon
Sugar according to taste
1 glass of Gin
Half a glass of Italian Vermouth

Shake well, strain into a tumbler and fill up with cold soda water.

Silver Fizz.

A gin fizz with the white of an egg in it.

Whisky Fizz.

Fill the shaker half full of broken ice and add:

The juice of half a lemon
Sugar according to taste
1 glass of Whisky

Shake well, strain into a tumbler and fill up with cold soda water.

Flips.

Flips belong to the same class of drinks as the egg noggs, but contain the yolk of a fresh egg and never any milk. The different flips are made of Sherry, Port, Claret, Vermouth, Whisky, Brandy etc.

Brandy Flip.

Fill the shaker half full of broken ice and add:

The yolk of a fresh egg
Sugar according to taste
One glass of Brandy

Shake well, strain into a small wine glass and add grated nutmeg on top.

Champagne Flip.

Fill the shaker half full of broken ice and add:

The yolk of a fresh egg
Sugar according to taste
Half a glass of Brandy

Shake well and strain into a large wine glass, fill up with Champagne and stir up.

Gin Flip.

Fill the shaker half full of broken ice and add:

The yolk of a fresh egg
Sugar according to taste
One glass of Dry Gin

Shake well, strain into a small wine glass and add grated nutmeg on top.

Sherry Flip.

Fill the shaker half full of broken ice and add:

The yolk of a fresh egg
Sugar syrup according to taste
One glass of Pale Dry Sherry

Shake well, strain into a small wine glass and add grated nutmeg on top.

Vermouth Flip.

Fill the shaker half full of broken ice and add

The yolk of a fresh egg
Sugar syrup according to taste
One glass of Italian Vermouth

Shake well, strain into a small wine glass and add grated nutmeg on top.

Whisky Flip.

Fill the shaker half full of broken ice and add:

The yolk of a fresh egg
Sugar according to taste
One glass of Whisky

Shake well, strain into a small wine glass and add grated nutmeg on top.

Long Drinks.

Canadian Rickey.

In a medium sized glass: the juice of one lime or half a lemon, a cocktail glass of Rye Whisky, a piece of ice, and fill up with Appollinaris or other mineral water.

Horses Neck.

Place the peel of a lemon in a tumbler with one end hanging over the top of glass, add two lumps of ice and fill the glass with cold Ginger ale.

John Collins.

Fill the shaker half full of broken ice and add:

The juice of one and a half lemon
Sugar according to taste
One and a half glass of Whisky

Shake well and pour this into a large bar glass and fill up with cold soda water, serve with straws.

Tom Collins.

Fill the shaker half full of broken ice and add:

The juice of one and a half lemon
Sugar according to taste
One and a half glass of Dry Gin

Shake well, pour into a large bar glass and fill with cold soda water. Serve with straws.

Punches.

Punches are numerous and various. They can be served either cold or hot. When served cold they are generally decorated with fruits in season, when served hot a slice of lemon on top is sufficient.

American Punch.
(4—6 persons)

Fill a stew pan with following ingredients:

4 pieces of sugar
1 little piece of cinnamon
Lemon peel
5 cloves
Half a wine glass of Whisky
Half a glass of Portwine
Two wine glasses of plain water

Let boil and serve in a tumbler.

Sours.

Brandy Sour.

Fill the shaker half full of broken ice and add:

The juice of a lemon
Sugar according to taste
1 glass of Brandy

Shake well, strain into a small tumbler and fill upp with cold soda water.

Claret Sour.

Fill the shaker half full of broken ice and add:

The juice of a lemon
Sugar according to taste
One and a half glass of Claret
Half a glass of Brandy

Shake well, strain into a small tumbler and fill up with plain water.

Derby Sour.

Fill the shaker half full of broken ice and add:

The juice of half a lemon
Sugar according to taste
1/3 of Rum
1/3 of Whisky
1/3 of Italian Vermouth

Shake well, strain into a small tumbler and fill up with cold soda water.

Manhattan Sour.

Fill the shaker half full of broken ice and add:

The juice of a lemon
1 glass of Rye Whisky
Half a glass of Italian Vermouth

Shake well, strain into a small tumbler and fill up with cold soda water.

Martini Sour.

Fill the shaker half full of broken ice and add:

The juice of a lemon
Sugar according to taste
1 glass of Gin
Half a glass of Italian Vermouth

Shake well and strain into a small tumbler and add a little splash of soda water on top.

Saratoga Sour.

Fill the shaker half full of broken ice and add:

The juice of half a lemon
Sugar according to taste
1 glass of Rye Whisky
3 dashes of Anisette
Half a glass of Dry Vermouth

Shake well, strain into a small tumbler and fill up with plain water.

Vermouth Sour.

Fill the shaker half full of broken ice and add:
The juice of a lemon
Sugar according to taste
One and a half glass of Italian Vermouth
Shake well, strain into a small tumbler and fill up with cold soda water.

Whisky Sour.

Fill the shaker half full of broken ice and add:
The juice of a lemon
Sugar according to taste
1 glass of Rye Whisky
Shake well, strain into a small tumbler and fill up with cold soda water.

Cups.

Castle Cup.
(12—14 persons)

Put a large piece of ice in a big jug and add:
2 bottles of Claret
2 bottles of Graves Wine
5 wine glasses of Brandy
2 bottles of Soda water
2 cocktail glasses of Brown Curacao
2 large peels of cucumber
Some grated nutmeg on top
Sugar according to taste
Stir up and serve in Champagne glasses.

Champagne Cup.

(4 persons)

Put a large lump of ice in a big jug and add:

1 liqueur glass of Cherry Brandy
1 liqueur glass of Curacao
2 liqueur glasses of Brandy
1 bottle of iced Champagne
1 bottle of cold soda water

Stir up well and decorate with different kinds of fruit in season. A sprig of fresh mint or a slice of cucumber peel is often added.

Claret Cup.

(4 persons)

The Claret cup is made in the same way as the Champagne Cup, but a little lemon juice instead of Cherry Brandy improves it.

Madeira Cup.

(4 persons)

Put a large piece of ice in a big jug and add:

The juice of two lemons
2 cocktail glasses of Italian Vermouth
1 bottle of Dry Madeira Wine
1 bottle of cold soda water

Stir up well and decorate with thinly cut slices of lemon, orange and pine-apple.

Punsch Cup.

(4 persons).

Put a large lump of ice in a glass can and add:

Half a bottle of Swedish Punsch
One bottle of Niersteiner Wine
Half a wine glass of Green Curacao

Stir well and serve in Champagne glasses.

_____

Toddies.

These drinks can be served hot or cold, by using respectively hot water or ice and cold water.

King's Toddy.

Dissolve three pieces of sugar in hot water and add:

> One cocktail glass of Claret
> Half a cocktail glass of Brandy
> One cocktail glass of Portwine

Fill up with boiling water, add a slice of lemon and serve with a bar spoon.

Portwine Toddy.

Dissolve four pieces of sugar in a tumbler and add:

> 1 wine glass full of Portwine

Fill up with boiling water, add a slice of lemon, serve with a bar spoon.

Rum Toddy.

Dissolve four pieces of sugar in a tumbler and add:

> One glass of Jamaica Rum

Fill up with boiling water, add two slices of lemon, serve with a bar spoon.

Stockholm Toddy.

Dissolve two pieces of sugar in a tumbler and add:

> Half a cocktail glass of Brandy
> Half a cocktail glass of Portwine
> 4 dashes of Raspberry syrup

Fill up with boiling water, add a slice of lemon, serve with a bar spoon.

Whisky Toddy.

Dissolve four pieces of sugar in a tumbler and add:

> One glass of Whisky

Fill up with boiling water, add a slice of lemon, serve with a bar spoon.

Glögg

(The Yule Tide Drink of Sweden)

A Christmas Holiday in Sweden without Glögg is almost unthinkable, it having been a custom for generations. It is always an event when the paraphernalia for blending Glögg, in the traditional manner, is assembled:—a copper kettle, a wire grill, a long handled ladle, and the following ingredients:

1 bottle Brandy
2 bottles Claret
2 bottles Port Wine
25 Cloves
20 Cardamon Seeds
1 lb. Sweet Almonds
   (blanched)
1 lb. Seedless Raisins
2 oz. Cinnamon Sticks
1 lb. Lump Sugar
2 oz. Dried Orange Peel
   (Pommeranze)

Put dried orange peel, cardamon seeds, cinnamon sticks and cloves in a cheese cloth bag and boil slowly in wine for 15 minutes. Add almonds, and raisins, and boil another 15 minutes. Remove kettle from stove, place wire grill over it with sugar on top, and gradually pour brandy over sugar. Hold a lighted match near sugar; brandy will flame up. When sugar is melted, remove grill. Extinguish flame by covering kettle. Remove bag of spices. Serve hot with a few almonds and raisins in each glass.

INDEX

INDEX

COCKTAILS

INDEX

FLIPS

LONG DRINKS

PUNCHES

SOURS

CUPS

TODDIES